AF573871

BISON
BOOKS

At Table series

Spiced

Recipes from Le Pré Verre

Philippe Delacourcelle

Translated & with a preface by Adele King & Bruce King

University of Nebraska Press · Lincoln and London

Library of Congress Cataloging-in-Publication Data
Delacourcelle, Philippe.
[Ma cuisine à fleur d'épices. English]
Spiced : recipes from Le Pré Verre / Philippe Delacourcelle ; translated and with a preface by Adele King and Bruce King.
p. cm.
Includes index.
ISBN 978-0-8032-6010-8 (pbk. : alk. paper)
1. Cookery, French. 2. Cookery (Spices). 3. Pré Verre (Restaurant). I. Pré Verre (Restaurant). II. Title.
TX719.D383 2007
641.5944—dc22 2007013361

Set in Minion by Kim Essman. Designed by A. Shahan.

This translation is dedicated to Marny Payne,
for her botanical knowledge and her friendship.

The translators also want to thank Jerry Tobias
for his careful reading of the manuscript,
and Lisa Kelly Boët for advice on sea salts.

Contents

Preface

Adele King & Bruce King

Spiced: Recipes from Le Pré Verre is an English translation of Philippe Delacourcelle's remarkable *Ma cuisine à fleur d'épices,* one of the more exciting cookbooks to appear in recent years. These original and easy-to-make recipes will take you directly into the mind (perhaps taste buds would be better) of one of the better cooks in France and what might be considered a new school of cooking in which spices replace or complement the herbs that have been so basic to French and most European cuisine. Delacourcelle might be thought of as belonging to the current fashion for "fusion" cuisine, but unlike many cooks who mix, match, and blend cuisines, he remains a French cook. His techniques and dishes are recognizably French but are usually accented with new flavors from around the globe. His green bean salad is the traditional French combination of beans, crème fraîche, shallot, and lemon but made into a great dish by the addition of lots of cilantro (fresh coriander). To the usual scallops in a butter and cream sauce he adds soy sauce. Fresh mackerel gets a soy glaze. His fresh tomato soup calls for grated coconut, lime juice, and various spices. His trout has a green tea sauce. Delacourcelle is not the first to use such spices, but the elegant simplicity of his recipes is eye-opening.

Philippe and his brother, Marc, are well known to the French restaurant scene. Philippe worked with several famous French chefs and worked in kitchens in Asia where he learned Chinese, Japanese, Malaysian, Indian, and other cuisines. Then in 1984 the two brothers opened Le Clos Morillons in the 15th arrondissement of Paris. Offering some of the finest fusion cuisine in France, it was awarded a mention in the *Michelin Guide* and kept its "mention" even after it was sold, as the new owner wisely retained many of Delacourcelle's recipes. In 2003 Delacourcelle opened Le Pré Verre in the heart of the

Latin Quarter, and it immediately became the new sensation, winning praise in both the French and foreign press. Patricia Wells, the *Fodor Guide*, and the *New York Times* recommended it. Although the food is definitely bistro in its excellence, the atmosphere is more like a brasserie, with much talk, people coming and going, friends meeting, even conversation between tables—very unlike the solemnity of most good French restaurants. In warm weather, tables overflow the sidewalks.

Philippe is a hands-on chef who is always in the kitchen cooking while Marc is in the front of the restaurant greeting customers and taking orders. Around 11 p.m., when most of the customers are leaving, Philippe wanders out of the kitchen and talks to those who remain. Many know him by now, as Le Pré Verre is a restaurant to which diners often return. Conversation is usually about the cooking, the unusual spices and flavors, the unexpected herbs that garnish plates and which Philippe has found in one of the two oriental groceries around the corner on Place Maubert. The leaves and flavors keep changing, evidence of Philippe's curiosity and inventiveness. The joy of discovery and experimentation and an air of informality can be found in the dishes here.

Besides offering a selection of or variations on the recipes included here, Le Pré Verre is inexpensive for Paris and offers good, affordable wines. Unlike those chefs who have tried for Michelin "stars" by making their restaurants more luxurious, using more expensive ingredients, hiring more staff, raising prices, and limiting the number of customers to one seating, Delacourcelle aims at having an inexpensive, popular bistro with a constant turnover of customers. It is always jammed full, reservations are essential, and even so there are often people waiting for others to finish their coffee. It is not the quietest restaurant in the world, but it feels lively. Even the basement is filled with diners. One night we asked Marc about them and he laughed, saying the basement was filled with a party from Michelin. With such customers he does not need to advertise.

Ma cuisine à fleur d'épices is almost as popular as Delacourcelle's restaurant. Everyone who is interested in cooking seems to have a copy. For French food it is surprisingly easy to make; the recipes do not demand the fancy cutting, elaborate techniques, or years of training that many French recipes from good chefs require. Nor do they require the chemicals and fancy equipment of the fashionable new school of Spanish "laboratory" cooking.

Delacourcelle belongs to an influential new group of Western European chefs who use spices instead of the traditional herbs of French and European cooking. His dishes make use of fenugreek, lime leaves (kaffir or combava), sumac, citronelle (lemongrass), Szechuan pepper, caraway seed, star anise, ginger, sesame seed and oil, soy sauce, vanilla, cumin, coriander seed, and various curry powder combinations. Loosely speaking these are oriental flavors, although they come from around the world: sumac is a biblical spice found in Middle Eastern cooking; ras el-hanout is a North African curry combination; Colombo is the French Caribbean curry; Maniguette is a West African pepper; allspice is from Jamaica; and Espelette pepper is a paprika from Spain and the south of France. Many of the spices were already part of European cookery, but caraway and poppy seeds, for example, are more common to Nordic countries, Eastern Europe, or the Mediterranean than to Paris, or were used rarely in French cuisine. Others, such as star anise, are from Chinese and Indian cuisine. Delacourcelle has brought such flavors to French cooking, often in new ways. The European herbs he uses, such as cilantro, were seldom the dominant flavors of previous northern French cooking.

Contemporary French cuisine is still responding to the changes brought about during the 1960s and 1970s by the New Cuisine and Thin Cuisine, which aimed to make French food more digestible and less fattening by reducing the amount of butter, cream, fats, and flour. There are now excellent chefs who only cook with oils and nonfat yogurt. Some chefs are influenced by the extraordinary "workshop" of El Bulli in Spain with its amazing and complicated transformations of ingredients into new physical states. Still others have tried to reclaim the traditional cuisine of "Grand-mère" with its fats and slow cooking, but in a more digestible way. Delacourcelle shares in all of these tendencies. His food still uses some butter, cream, and even flour (usually a little corn starch like the Asians), but in small quantities. He often uses flavored oils. Although his cooking requires no complicated techniques, some of the dishes are produced in such unexpected ways that they could easily be considered the product of an avant-garde workshop. His "Two-sesame chocolate cream" is a delight to look at, easy to make, and radically different from any other recipe we know. "Duck legs cooked with tea and cinnamon" sounds strange but is both easy and marvelous. Like "Green beans with coriander" and "Two-sesame chocolate cream," it is a dish for which guests always request the recipe. Essentially he has reinvigorated traditional French food by using hints from other cuisines, especially by using spices and herbs differently. Delacourcelle is idiosyncratic; a few dishes (such as "Spinach with nutmeg") are traditionally French but included here because they use spice. Sometimes the source is obvious, such as Japanese soy sauce or the French Caribbean curry known as Colombo. "Grilled chicken breasts with ginger" is a simplified version of Japanese yakitori brochettes.

Although translating from one language and culture to another requires some adaptation, we have kept close to Delacourcelle's original recipe, only substituting American weights, measurements, and cooking terms. We have added notes at the end of recipes in which we suggest possible substitutions of ingredients, identify different ways of cooking or using a recipe, and warn of possible problems. The "Spicy fish stew," for example, tastes and looks beautiful, but unless it is served in large, flat soup bowls it will be difficult to eat without breaking up the fish first. This stew uses a marvelous combination of salt and spices, which we now always keep handy on our table to use at many meals. You might consider it a separate recipe for a flavored salt.

While most of the ingredients will be available at large supermarkets, others can be found at gourmet and ethnic food stores. With its large ethnic population and ethnic restaurants, the United States often acculturates foreign foods long before France does. Americans are also more used to strong spices and hot peppers than the French are. Only a few ingredients here will be difficult to find, and a computer search or a few telephone calls to ethnic shops will produce results. Delacourcelle likes to use different curry combinations, different kinds of peppers, spices that can be found in Parisian spice shops. Many of his "exotic" spices are now common in the United States and have become part of its ethnic and multicultural cuisine. Don't panic if you lack some of the spices: Delacourcelle often indicates substitutes, and we have suggested others. Using this book will inspire you to buy new and different spices. Since the French prefer lightly spiced food, you might want to increase the amount of spices. (A French friend asked if we found the Creole food of New Orleans too spicy.) The idea is to make the food interesting and tasty but not overwhelmed by spices. You will also learn some of the basics of good cooking, such as how to use ice water to stop vegetables from overcooking, how to beat egg whites, and how to keep milk from boiling over. The "Seasonings" section will give you sauces and salsas to improve many simple dishes.

French recipes in the not-too-distant past were more likely to list ingredients than to give precise details about measurements and cooking. While Delacourcelle is more modern in offering good instructions for how to make his dishes, his recipes reflect his experience as a working chef. When we told him we were going to add comments based our experience in using his recipes, he approved, saying that recipes are only a starting point. Many of the recipes here appear on the Pré Verre menu in slightly different forms according to what is available at the time. We urge you to take a similar approach. Delacourcelle is a marvelous cook, and he gets the balance between ingredients right more often than most chefs do. The recipes are excellent, but you can also use them as a source for new ideas for varying your own cooking with spices.

Always use fresh ingredients. One reason the food at Le Pré Verre tastes so good is that Delacourcelle buys high-quality spices that are freshly ground or which he grinds himself. Store-bought spices lose their flavors over time. Also use local ingredients. The rascasse in "Scorpion fish with fennel" is a common fish in Europe. A kind of ocean perch, it is known in English as a scorpion fish and is available in California. It is similar to the more common redfish, and frankly, fresh red snapper is as good or better.

There are more fish, fowl, and vegetable dishes here than red meat dishes because that is what is fashionable as Parisians have become aware of healthy eating. There are few beef dishes, since beef is less popular in France since the mad cow scare. Besides, the French have always liked lamb, veal, and pork. There are several pumpkin recipes, as both the larger and smaller varieties of pumpkin have been rediscovered by French cooks. Sweet potatoes are also in fashion. *Ma cuisine* is both an introduction to the cooking of one of the more inventive chefs in Paris and also a sampling of what has become trendy eating on both sides of the Atlantic.

Consult Delacourcelle's "Description of Spices" for comments about spices, including fascinating information about their history. Following the list of spices we have given some suggestions for possible substitutions for French salts, cream, and potatoes.

We have converted French weights into pounds and ounces, and also cups and spoons. (The designation "ounce" always refers to weight, not volume.) We have also included metric measurements in grams. Volume is given in cups and tablespoons and also in centiliters. (An American cup is 24 centiliters, and a tablespoon is 1.5 centiliters.) Where exact measurements are not essential, we sometimes give approximate numbers. You might find a kitchen scale useful.

Ma cuisine à fleur d'épices lists specific French wines to go with each recipe. As most would not be readily available in the United States, and as they are not essential to the recipes, we have not included them. As Delacourcelle says in his introduction, however, wine accompanies these dishes well. Robust, aromatic wines (of which there are many American varieties) are best.

Introduction

Philippe Delacourcelle

What led a young French cook with traditional training to dust our culinary classics with spices and exotic aromas to give them refined and original accents? I know that what I did is not at all common in the world of chefs. I am not aiming to overthrow tradition in the kitchen but to change the angle of vision, to aim our sights in a different direction. For each recipe I have tried to heighten a dish in our repertoire or a classic ingredient in our markets by unexpected means, to give a new tonality to a dish that we thought we knew. I love to reproduce, in a dish, by precise amounts, the particular charm that the spices have for me. In my travels, from the lessons I have learned from enchanting tastes I met along the way, I have drawn the quintessence; the spices have taught me a language that I have applied, with passion, to my work—by finding the right ingredient, the right quantity, the right moment. I had classic training as a cook and a pastry cook. Later I worked as pastry chef at Fauchon's, then as a chef in various gourmet restaurants, and especially at the restaurant of Bernard Loiseau in Saulieu, where I was the second chef. I have always been attracted by foreign cuisines, particularly those of Southeast Asia. In restaurant kitchens I worked alongside Japanese cooks who loved good food and refinement of taste. In 1979 I undertook a long trip out of France to study the cuisines of eastern Asia. For five years I traveled around these regions, beginning in Japan, where I met friends who were pleased to guide me in my gastronomic quest. Next it was in Malaysia and Singapore, which remain somewhat my favorites because of their culinary richness and their love of life. After that I went to Indonesia, to Thailand, to Hong Kong, to Korea, and more recently to China. Naturally, when I came back to France I tried to reproduce the magic flavors that I found during my travels.

Since 1984, the year I opened my restaurant Le Clos Morillons in the 15th arrondissement of Paris, I have continued this research. The success of my blends of spices encouraged me to write simple recipes, based on ordinary ingredients, that could be used by gourmets who are not necessarily experts in the culinary arts.

In my approach, I do not try to imitate oriental cuisines or to make French dishes unrecognizable; instead, I add ingredients and tricks from overseas to the base of our culinary tradition in order to create a new feeling, a new accent. It is a fascinating game that heightens and lightens the flavors, accentuating their poetry and their potential to make us dream. Depending on the way I use it, the spice accompanies the dish in different ways: sometimes deep, subtle aromas are created by long cooking; at other times, fireworks of flavors, added at the last minute, burst forth in a surprising fashion. Often adding a spice to a simple preparation (apple tart, vinaigrette, lamb stew) introduces an unexpected note, but the basic product, the theme of the dish, is always present and intact. In the recipes that follow, only the spices bring an exotic touch. The technique is indeed French, and the basic products can be found regularly in our shops, markets, and supermarkets. Similarly, most of the spices are not difficult to find. Pepper, nutmeg, cinnamon, clove, curry, cumin, caraway, vanilla, saffron, and allspice are found everywhere. Ginger, star anise, cardamom, coriander, turmeric, and anise are only slightly less common. As for lemongrass, lime leaves, long pepper, Maniguette pepper, Szechuan pepper, tonka bean, garam masala, and other mixtures of spices, most can be found in Asian supermarkets, which are more and more common in France. In addition, I often give possible substitutions of flavor in case you cannot find the spices I initially suggest.

How to accompany these dishes? A commonplace idea is that spices are difficult to match with wines. It's not so simple! The Chinese have always appreciated grape wines of central Asia in their aromatic cuisine. It is pointless to make do with beer or the eternal rosé de Provence. Red or white? What matters is that the bouquet of the wine completes the accents of the spices, is complementary to them without necessarily resembling them. The flavors should be complex, and wine, especially white wine, should have a robust, honeyed, aromatic base. Mellow wine, not too sweet or coarse, is always welcome. It should have character in order to play its part in the spicy symphony. Among the Loire valley wines (which I particularly like because of my origins), I like the Vouvrays, the Savennières, the Anjou whites; Alsatian wines (Gewürztraminer, of course, but also Tokay, Riesling, etc.) are valuable, as are the wines of the southwest, of the lower Rhone valley, and of the south, often in perfect harmony with the spicy flavors. The Chardonnay variety, as long as it is not too woody, and the marvelous Viognier variety, from the Rhone and the south, can produce intense and magic marriages of flavors. I invite you to discover this cooking touched with spices: the trip will not take you far from your familiar base, but you will make many surprising discoveries.

Spiced

1 Terrines

Terrine of rabbit, eggplant, and fenugreek
Terrine de lapin à l'aubergine, et au fenugrec

SERVES 8 TO 10	PREPARATION: 1 hour COOKING: 1 hour 15 minutes REFRIGERATION: 12 hours

- 1 rabbit
- 1 pound (400 grams) streaky smoked bacon, without rind, sliced thin
- 3 eggplants
- 1 tablespoon fenugreek seeds (or mustard seeds)
- Fine salt, freshly ground white pepper, fleur de sel

Debone the rabbit.

Heat the oven to 350°F (180°C).

Line a terrine dish 12 inches (25 cm) long and 4 inches (8 cm) tall with the bacon slices. The bacon slices should be higher than the dish so they can be folded over the rabbit.

With a serrated knife, cut the eggplants lengthwise in ½-inch (1 cm) slices. Then cut in half so they fit the terrine dish.

In a small pan, boil a little water with the fenugreek seeds for a minute and let them cool in the water.

Place a layer of raw eggplant in the bottom of the terrine dish, and season with fine salt and pepper. Spread on this layer half of the rabbit, seasoned with half of the fenugreek. Cover with another layer of eggplant, then the rest of the rabbit and the fenugreek. Finish with a last layer of eggplant, and cover the terrine by folding down the bacon slices.

Cook the terrine in a bain-marie in the oven for 1 hour 15 minutes. Remove from the oven and add a weight covered with aluminum foil. Let it cool for 2 hours, then refrigerate, with the weight in place, for 12 hours.

To unmold hold the terrine slightly tilted under hot water for 30 seconds. Then turn out on a plate and add fleur de sel and pepper.

CHEF'S COMMENTS: Fenugreek is normally used with vegetables. In this recipe it adds an original, surprising touch of licorice.

Chicken or another fowl might be substituted for rabbit.—**TRANS.**

BAIN-MARIE: A bain-marie is a pan of hot water into which you put terrine molds, dessert molds, etc. and then bake them in the oven surrounded by the hot water.

Terrine of lentils, preserved duck gizzards, and ras el-hanout

Terrine de lentilles et gésiers confits au ras el-hanout

SERVES 6 TO 8	PREPARATION: 15 minutes COOKING: 20 minutes REFRIGERATION: about 8 hours

12-ounce (350 g) can of preserved duck gizzards
½ pound (200 g) green Puy lentils, rinsed and drained
½ onion
½ carrot
½ stalk of celery
1 sprig thyme
1 bay leaf
1 tablespoon ras el-hanout (or curry)
1 cup (25 cl) of whipping (heavy) cream
2½ envelopes unflavored gelatin (equivalent to 17 g, 12 leaves of gelatin)
Salt, freshly ground pepper

Drain the gizzards, keeping the fat. Peel, wash, and coarsely chop the vegetables. In a pan, brown the vegetables over low heat for 1 minute in a bit of duck fat. Add the lentils, thyme, and bay leaf and moisten with 4 cups (1 liter) water. Cook for 20 minutes over low heat. Remove the vegetables. Drain the lentils in a sieve and refrigerate.

Soak the gelatin in cold water. Heat ½ teaspoon duck fat with the ras el-hanout for 15 seconds, add the cream, and bring to a boil. Remove from the heat and incorporate the drained gelatin with a whisk. Let it cool.

In a bowl, mix the cold lentils, the gizzards, and the cold cream. Add salt and pepper. Line the interior of a terrine dish with aluminum foil or plastic wrap, then add the mixture and refrigerate for about 8 hours.

Unmold the terrine, cut it in very thin slices, and arrange these in a fan shape on a dish. You can accompany this terrine with a spicy condiment or chutney.

CHEF'S COMMENTS: In this mixture of flavors, the ras el-hanout brings France to the gates of Morocco.

Duck gizzards are less common in the United States than in France. If you cannot find a can of duck gizzards, try this recipe with dark meat of duck.—**TRANS.**

Terrine of duck and green peppercorns

Terrine de canard au poivre vert

SERVES 6	PREPARATION: 30 minutes COOKING: 1 hour REFRIGERATION: 12 hours

6 deboned duck legs
1 egg
6 bay leaves
1 tablespoon green peppercorns
Salt, freshly ground white pepper

Preheat the oven to 350°F (180°C).

Put the duck meat through a meat grinder or food processor, without removing the skin or fat. Add the egg and the seasonings, and mix with a wooden spatula. Taste and adjust the seasoning (but don't eat the raw duck!). Put the mixture in a mold or terrine dish, and cover the surface with bay leaves. Cook in a bain-marie for 1 hour. Remove from the oven and cover with a weight, pressing down for a few seconds. Let it cool for 2 hours, then refrigerate overnight, still covered with the weight.

Serve the next day in its mold. You can accompany the terrine with a sweet aubergine chutney, for example, or cut it in thin slices arranged on a bed of salad dressed with walnut oil.

CHEF'S COMMENTS: This is a terrine of surprising simplicity, with a spicy taste of duck and green pepper. It is classic but delicious.

Too often in France, terrines are bound together with pork or veal.—**TRANS.**

Calf's head with Chinese spices
Fromage de tête de veau aux épices chinoises

SERVES 6	PREPARATION: 20 to 30 minutes COOKING: 2 hours REFRIGERATION: 12 hours

½ calf's head
½ calf's tongue
3 carrots, peeled
1 onion, peeled
1 leek (only the white part)
6 star anise
1 stick of cassia (Chinese cinnamon)
1 tablespoon Szechuan pepper
2 envelopes unflavored gelatin (equivalent to 14 g, 10 leaves of gelatin)
3 tablespoons finely chopped parsley
6 tablespoons peanut oil
3 tablespoons sherry vinegar
Fine salt, coarse sea salt

Put the calf's head and tongue, 1 carrot, onion, leek, cinnamon, and star anise in a pot. Cover with water, bring to a boil, and cook for 2 hours over low heat.

During this time, cook 2 carrots in water with sea salt. Watch the cooking to be sure they don't get too soft.

Drain the calf's head and tongue, cut into 1-inch (2 to 3 cm) pieces, put in a bowl, and season with fine salt and ground Szechuan pepper.

Put the cooking liquid through a sieve, then cook to →

reduce by half. Soak the gelatin for a few minutes in cold water, then add to the cooking liquid. Add a little salt and Szechuan pepper.

Mix together in a terrine dish, keeping the whole carrots in the middle. Refrigerate for 12 hours.

Before serving, mix the parsley, oil, vinegar, and a little salt in a blender. Cut the terrine in thick slices and season with the vinaigrette.

CHEF'S COMMENTS: This is an irresistible version of calf's head, with some Chinese flavors.

Cinnamon could replace Chinese cinnamon.—**TRANS.**

Terrine of green peas and sumac
Terrine de petits pois au sumac

SERVES 6 TO 8

PREPARATION: 1 hour
COOKING: 10 minutes
REFRIGERATION: about 5 hours

- 5 pounds (2.5 kg) fresh green peas, shelled
- 1 tablespoon ras el-hanout (or substitute curry)
- 2 tablespoons sumac (or substitute paprika)
- 1½ cups (40 cl) whipping (heavy) cream
- 3 envelopes unflavored gelatin (equivalent to 21 g, 15 leaves of gelatin)
- 6 tablespoons olive oil
- 2 tablespoons sherry vinegar
- Fine salt, coarse sea salt

Plunge the peas into boiling water, seasoned with coarse sea salt, and cook for 8 minutes. (If you like them very tender, cook 3 minutes longer.)

Drain the peas; plunge them immediately into a bowl of cold water. Cool for 15 minutes, then drain.

Soak the gelatin for 5 minutes in cold water. Heat the cream with the ras el-hanout, bring to a boil, and add salt. Off the heat, mix in the drained gelatin with a whisk. Set aside.

Line a terrine dish with plastic wrap. Add the peas, then cover them with the cream. Refrigerate for about 5 hours. To serve, mix the olive oil, vinegar, salt, and 1 tablespoon of sumac. Unmold the terrine and cut in ½-inch (1 cm) slices. Arrange the slices on plates, moisten with the vinaigrette, and dust with sumac. →

CHEF'S COMMENTS: The peas are coated with sweet spices: everything depends on the delicacy of the taste. In this recipe the acidity and fruitiness of the sumac blends well with the peas.

At Le Pré Verre, vegetable terrines are often used as a foundation, garnished with shrimp or other seafood.—**TRANS.**

Terrine of chicken, sorrel, and Moroccan spices
Terrine de poulette à l'oseille, et au ras el-hanout

SERVES 6 TO 8	PREPARATION: 50 minutes COOKING: 1 hour 15 minutes REFRIGERATION: 6 hours

1 young chicken, about 2½ pounds (1.2 kg), cleaned, with neck and feet removed
¾ pound (300 g) sorrel
1 carrot, peeled
½ stalk of celery, peeled
½ white of leek
1 onion, peeled
2 cloves
1 star anise
½ stick cinnamon
½ teaspoon ras el-hanout (or curry)
¾ cup (150 g, 6 oz) butter
2½ envelopes unflavored gelatin (equivalent to 17 g, 12 leaves of gelatin)
Coarse salt, fine salt

Cut the carrot, celery, and leek into 1-inch (2 cm) pieces. Cut the onion in half and add a clove to each half.

Rinse the chicken. Put it in a pan with the vegetables, the cinnamon, star anise, and a pinch of coarse salt. Cover and cook for 1 hour 15 minutes at a slow boil.

Tail and wash the sorrel. (If it is sandy, wash it 3 times, shaking well to make the sand fall off.) Dry it and cook for 5 minutes in a covered pot. Drain in a sieve. Set aside. →

Debone the cooked chicken and cut the meat into ½-inch (1 cm) pieces. Soak the gelatin in cold water. Mix the chicken with the sorrel.

Boil ¾ cup (20 cl) of the stock from the chicken with the ras el-hanout. Off the, heat add the gelatin and the butter. Mix well, check the seasoning.

Pour this sauce on the chicken and mix well. Line a terrine dish with plastic wrap and refrigerate for 6 hours. Unmold and cut in thick slices.

CHEF'S COMMENTS: The acidity of the sorrel and the tenderness of the chicken highlight the flavors in the ras el-hanout. You can individualize your spice mixture as you like, adding powdered ginger or coriander, even cumin.

Spinach could be used instead of sorrel.—**TRANS.**

2 Cold Starters

Skate marinated with lemongrass
Marinade de raie à la citronnelle crue

SERVES 4 | PREPARATION: 30 minutes
COOKING: 20 minutes

18 ounces (500 g) skate
1 ounce (25 g) cooked beet
½ bulb of fennel
1 onion
1 sprig thyme
1 bunch chives
1 bay leaf
2 stalks lemongrass
Juice of half a lemon
6 tablespoons (10 cl) olive oil
Fine salt, coarse sea salt, fleur de sel

Put the skate, peeled onion, thyme, bay leaf, and a pinch of coarse sea salt in a large pan. Cover with water. Cut the lemongrass stalks in two, reserving an inch or two of bulb, and put the rest in the pot. Bring to a simmer and cook for 20 minutes.

Remove the fish with a slotted spoon. Take off the skin, and separate the flesh from the bones. Spread it, fan-shaped, on a serving plate (or individual plates). Keep it warm.

Blend for 1 minute the beet, lemon juice, olive oil, and a pinch of salt.

Cut the fennel and the remaining lemongrass bulb into small dice, as thin as possible. Cut the chives with scissors. Put the sauce on the fish, add fennel, chives, lemongrass, and a little fleur de sel.

CHEF'S COMMENTS: Lemongrass is very popular in Thailand. Lemongrass quickly brings back many taste memories for me. It is used in France raw like a shallot: the result is different, more European. Try a lot of it on all sorts of salads.

The French love skate. Those who do not might make this dish with shark or possibly squid or octopus, cooking much less.—**TRANS.**

Salad of wild rice, mango, basil, and star anise
Salade de riz sauvage, mangue, basilic, et badiane

SERVES 4	PREPARATION: 15 minutes COOKING: 1 hour SOAKING: 2 to 3 hours

½ pound (200 g) wild rice
1 ripe tomato
1 ripe mango
1 small onion
1 bunch of fresh basil
2 pinches of powdered star anise
3 tablespoons (5 cl) olive oil
2 teaspoons (1 cl) sherry vinegar
Salt, freshly ground white pepper

Soak the wild rice for 2 to 3 hours. Cook it covered for 40 minutes over low heat in 2½ times its volume of water. Let it puff up off the heat, still covered, then cool it in a bowl.

Cut the mango in half lengthwise, with your knife against the sides of the mango stone. Cut the mango into ½-inch (1 cm) dice.

Peel the onion and chop coarsely. Cut the tomato into small dice. Cut the basil leaves coarsely.

In the salad bowl, mix the oil, vinegar, and star anise powder. Add salt and white pepper, then the rice, the mango, the tomato, and the onion. Adjust the seasoning. If you like a more vinegary salad, add another tablespoon of vinegar.

Serve right away to take advantage of the flavors, which are rather fleeting.

CHEF'S COMMENTS: This flavorful salad can be eaten in all seasons. For formal dinners you can add lobster or crayfish tail, or even crab or shrimp. The powdered star anise seed underlines the exotic flavor of the mango. You can replace it with ½ teaspoon of another spice powder.

To get powdered star anise, grind whole star anise in a mortar or blender. Cut basil with scissors to avoid bruising the leaves.—**TRANS.**

Soft-boiled eggs with Szechuan pepper
Oeufs à la coque au poivre du Sichuan

SERVES 1	PREPARATION: 2 minutes COOKING: 3 to 4 minutes

1 to 2 eggs
Szechuan pepper in a pepper mill
Sel de Guérande, or another sea salt

Grind the sea salt in a mortar. Grind ½ teaspoon of Szechuan pepper and add to the salt.

Cook the eggs. To keep them from cracking in the boiling water, be sure they begin at room temperature. As soon as the water boils, lower the heat, then add the eggs. Raise the temperature moderately and cook 3 to 4 minutes, according to your taste.

Take the eggs off the heat and rinse them quickly in cold running water. Put them in a towel to keep the heat in.

When serving, cut the top of the eggs and sprinkle with the salt and pepper mixture.

CHEF'S COMMENTS: Nothing is simpler, but this aromatic mixture is a real marvel.

You can also grind sea salt in a salt mill. Be sure to use dry salt so as not to clog the mill. We keep one pepper mill filled with Szechuan peppercorns on hand. Soft-boiled eggs go well with chives, brown butter, and much else.—**TRANS.**

Melon with a spiced ice

Melon frappé au granité d'épices

SERVES 4	PREPARATION: 10 minutes COOKING: 2 minutes FREEZING: at least 12 hours

4 small ripe melons
Juice of ½ orange
Juice of ½ lemon
Pinch of powdered cinnamon
Pinch of powdered ginger
Pinch of powdered coriander
2 cups (50 cl) red wine
8 tablespoons (4 oz, 100 g) sugar

Put the sugar, 6 tablespoons (10 cl) of water, and the spices in a small pan and bring to a boil.

Mix the wine, spiced syrup, and fruit juices. Boil for 1 minute. Pour through a fine sieve into a shallow dish; there should only be about ½ inch (1 cm) of liquid. Put into the freezer and whisk every hour until crystals form. The liquid should become completely crystallized. Leave in the freezer overnight.

The next day, cut the melons in half, remove the seeds, and add the ice. Serve immediately, as the ice melts quickly.

CHEF'S COMMENTS: When it is 100 degrees in the shade, one's appetite often disappears. Thanks to the flavors of the spices, this dish will refresh and reinvigorate you.

Flavored ices can make many dishes more interesting. This spiced ice could be used with soft fruit for a dessert.—**TRANS.**

Celeriac with curry
Rémoulade de céleri au cari

SERVES 4

PREPARATION: 15 minutes
REFRIGERATION: 10 minutes

- ½ bulb of celeriac (celery root)
- Juice of ½ lemon
- ½ teaspoon curry powder
- 1 tablespoon mustard
- 4 tablespoons thick crème fraîche
- Fine salt

Peel the celeriac with a heavy knife, then grate it coarsely with a food processor. Mix the mustard, curry, crème fraîche, and lemon juice in a bowl. Add salt and the celeriac. Refrigerate for 10 minutes before serving.

CHEF'S COMMENTS: This rémoulade with curry is, for me, an improvement on the traditional rémoulade with mayonnaise.

Celeriac or celery root is more common to European than American cuisine, and should be used more. It makes a nice puree like mashed potatoes, or it can be added to stews. It cooks rapidly. We also like to serve celery rémoulade with cold or smoked salmon, cold roast turkey, cold chicken, etc.—**TRANS.**

Artichokes in a lemongrass sauce

Artichauts bretons, vinaigrette à la citronelle

SERVES 4

PREPARATION: 15 minutes
COOKING: 30 minutes

- 4 artichokes
- 4 lemons
- 6 kaffir lime leaves (or 3 stalks of lemongrass)
- 1 stalk of lemongrass
- Pinch of ground Szechuan pepper
- ¾ cup (20 cl) olive oil
- Fine salt, coarse salt

Squeeze 2 of the lemons. Remove the stalks of the artichokes. Cover them with water, add the lemon juice, a little coarse salt, and kaffir lime leaves, and cook at a slow boil for 20 to 30 minutes, depending on the size of the artichokes.

Prepare the vinaigrette. Use only the bulb of the lemongrass, cut it in thin rounds, then chop. Squeeze the two remaining lemons and sieve the juice to remove the seeds. Combine the oil and lemon juice, then add salt, Szechuan pepper, and the lemongrass. Set aside.

When the artichokes are cooked, turn them over to drain them well. Put the vinaigrette in 4 small bowls.

Eat the artichokes leaf by leaf, seasoning each with the vinaigrette. If you prepare this dish in advance, take the artichokes out of the refrigerator 1 hour before serving.

CHEF'S COMMENTS: The aroma of the kaffir lime highlights the slightly bitter taste of the artichokes. Here a flavor from a foreign land is added to a typical product of Brittany to produce a refreshing taste.

→

Cut off ⅛ inch of the top of the artichokes, and also remove the points on the leaves with scissors before cooking. You can also eat the stalks, split in two and cooked with the rest of the artichoke. If you don't have kaffir lime or lemongrass, cook the artichokes with extra lemon juice, not as fine a flavor, but a reasonable substitute. (Breton artichokes are small, with purple on the leaves.)—**TRANS.**

Tomatoes and mozzarella in ginger oil
Tomates-mozzarella à l'huile de gingembre

SERVES 4 | PREPARATION: 10 minutes

- 6 ripe tomatoes
- ½ pound (200 g) mozzarella
- 4 ounces (100 g) fresh ginger, about a 6-inch piece
- ½ teaspoon black sesame seeds
- Juice of ½ a lemon
- 6 tablespoons (10 cl) peanut oil
- Fine salt, freshly ground pepper

Plunge the tomatoes in boiling water for a few seconds, drain, peel, and cut into thin rounds. Cut the mozzarella into ½-inch (1 cm) dice. Peel and finely grate the ginger, and press the pulp in your hand to extract all the juice. Set the juice aside.

In a bowl mix the oil, the lemon juice, the ginger juice, the sesame seeds, and salt and pepper. You should have a ratio of ⅓ juice to ⅔ oil. Put the tomato slices in a serving dish and sprinkle with the mozzarella squares. Spoon the sauce over the dish, and leave for a few minutes before serving.

CHEF'S COMMENTS: Be sure to let the dish stand after seasoning to allow the ginger flavor to penetrate the tomatoes and mozzarella. Its peppery and acid accents are a delicious alternative to vinegar.

A garlic press can be used to extract the ginger juice rather than squeezing the pulp in your hands.—**TRANS.**

Romaine lettuce and smoked salmon with caraway seeds

Côtes de romaine au carvi et au saumon fumé

SERVES 4

PREPARATION: 30 minutes
COOKING: 1 minute

4 slices of Scottish smoked salmon
2 heads of tender green romaine lettuce
Juice of ½ lemon
1 shallot
1 sprig of dill
1 tablespoon caraway seeds
3 tablespoons thick crème fraîche
Salt, freshly ground white pepper

Cut off the base of the romaine lettuces. Trim each leaf, leaving about ½ inch (1 cm) of green on each side of the middle rib. Wash the lettuce and dry in a towel.

Put the caraway seeds in a small pan with a cup of water. Bring to a boil, then let cool for 30 minutes. Drain.

Chop the shallot finely. In a large salad bowl, mix the crème fraîche, shallot, caraway seeds, and lemon juice. Cover the romaine leaves with the sauce, and add salt and pepper.

Cut the salmon into 1-inch (2 cm) dice.

Place the romaine leaves in the plates, building them up two by two in three layers (not more, or they might collapse). Sprinkle with the salmon and dill leaves.

CHEF'S COMMENTS: This salad is an architectural creation on a plate. The romaine leaves are crunchy, and the caraway seeds add a hint of licorice.

A few caraway seeds make a nice, unexpected addition to most salads.—**TRANS.**

Green bean salad with cilantro

Salade de haricots verts à la coriandre fraîche

SERVES 4	PREPARATION: 20 minutes COOKING: 10 minutes

28 ounces (800 g) thin green beans
2 shallots
1 bunch cilantro
Juice of ½ lemon
3 tablespoons crème fraîche
Fine salt, rock salt, freshly ground pepper

Tail the green beans. In a large pot bring 8 cups of water to a boil with 1½ tablespoons (1 oz, 20 g) of rock salt. Prepare a bowl with cold water and ice cubes. When the water boils, add the beans and cook for 10 minutes after the water reboils. The beans should remain crisp. Take the pan from the heat and plunge the beans in the ice water, then drain, so that they are dry.

In a small bowl, mix the crème fraîche and lemon juice. Wash the cilantro leaves and dry in a paper towel. Chop finely. Chop the shallots finely. Mix these ingredients with the lemon and cream, and season. Then add the green beans.

CHEF'S COMMENTS: Cilantro has an intense flavor.

While a few leaves are enough for most dishes, we like the contrast between the beans and the bunch of cilantro here.—**TRANS.**

Salad of baby squid in toasted sesame oil
Salade tiède d'encornets à l'huile de sésame grillé

SERVES 6	PREPARATION: 5 minutes COOKING: 25 minutes

- 2¼ pounds (1 kg) squid weighing about ½ pound (200 g) each
- 1 bulb fennel
- 1 sprig thyme
- 1 bay leaf
- 6 tablespoons (10 cl) dry Sauvignon Blanc (or another dry white wine)
- 1 tomato
- 1 shallot
- 2 tablespoons toasted sesame oil
- 2 tablespoons peanut oil
- 1 tablespoon sherry vinegar
- Coarse salt, fine salt, freshly ground pepper

Get your fish merchant to clean the squid (if this is not possible, remove the gray skin with a grater, then clean out and remove the beak, which is very hard). Cut the bodies into rounds, and slice the tentacles in half.

Bring 1 quart (1 liter) of water, with a pinch of coarse salt, to a boil. Cut the cleaned fennel in half lengthwise, then cut each piece in very thin slices. Blanch the sliced fennel for 30 seconds and refresh in cold water, draining in a sieve and then drying on paper towels. To the fennel cooking water add the white wine, thyme, bay leaf, and the squid. Bring to a boil and cook for 25 minutes, then drain.

→

Chop the shallot. Cut the tomato into dice. Combine the oils, vinegar, fennel, squid, shallot, and tomato in a salad bowl. Mix well and season.

CHEF'S COMMENTS: This salad can be served warm or cold. The flavor of toasted sesame oil will transport you to the other side of the planet.

The fennel often found in shops has long stems and bruised or discolored outside portions. We remove them and use the tender bulb in salads and dishes such as this. We sweat the discarded parts in a pot with an onion and a clove of garlic until soft, then add water and maybe a chicken cube to make a nice soup that can be served hot or cold.—**TRANS.**

Marinated mackerel in soy sauce and ginger
Escabèche de maquereaux au soja et au gingembre

SERVES 4	PREPARATION: 15 minutes COOKING: 1 minute MARINATING: 5 hours

- 4 mackerels weighing ½ pound (200 g) each
- Juice of 1 lime
- 1 bunch of cilantro
- 2 ounces (50 g) fresh ginger, about a 3-inch piece
- 6 tablespoons (10 cl) soy sauce
- 6 tablespoons (10 cl) Japanese rice vinegar
- ½ teaspoon sugar

Have the mackerels filleted. Gently run your fingers along the fish to feel the small bones on the flesh side of each fillet, and remove them with a tweezers. This is not complicated and makes eating the mackerel more pleasant.

Peel and grate the ginger. Combine the vinegar, lime juice, soy sauce, ginger, sugar, and 1½ cups (40 cl) water in a small pan. Bring to a boil, then set aside.

Place cilantro on the bottom of a gratin dish. Top it with the mackerel, skin side down. When the marinade is warm, pour it gently on the fish. The liquid should completely cover the fish. Cover and refrigerate for 5 hours.

Drain the fillets, sieve the marinade, and take out the cilantro branches, which you will use to decorate each filet.

CHEF'S COMMENTS: Halfway between the Mediterranean tradition and Japanese cuisine, this recipe is a real treat →

in summer. You can accompany it with a salad of peppers or eggplant. The ginger adds freshness to the marinade.

Sherry vinegar or a white wine vinegar could be substituted for the rice vinegar. We love this simple dish. We make it with mackerel, sardines, or small red mullets.—**TRANS.**

Tuna pâté with dill and four peppers
Rilletes de thon à l'aneth et aux quatre poivres

SERVES 6 TO 8

PREPARATION: 20 minutes
COOKING: 10 minutes
REFRIGERATION: 3 hours

- 1½ pounds (600 g) fresh tuna, trimmed
- 1 bunch of fresh dill
- 2 shallots
- 10 Szechuan peppercorns
- 5 allspice berries
- 5 rose peppercorns
- 10 Maniguette (West African pepper) corns
- 1 cup (8 oz, 200 g) butter
- 3 tablespoons (5 cl) olive oil
- Juice of 1 lemon
- Fine salt

Peel the shallots and chop finely. Wash, dry, and chop the dill. Cut the tuna into 1-inch (2 cm) dice. Cut the butter into small pieces and work it with a fork to soften it. In a food processor, blender, or coffee mill, grind the four peppers finely.

In a frying pan, gently heat the olive oil. Add the shallots and cook for 1 minute. Add the tuna and cook, stirring carefully; the tuna should stay red in the center. Let this cool. Add the other ingredients and mix with a wooden spatula to obtain a smooth paste. Add the juice of the lemon, and salt as needed.

Line a terrine dish or a plastic container with plastic wrap, add the pâté, and refrigerate for 2 to 3 hours. →

CHEF'S COMMENTS: This is a tasty first course, easy to keep and easy to serve. The variety of peppers gives a refreshing flavor to the tuna.

Black and green peppercorns could be substituted for the four peppers, though they have less exotic flavor.—**TRANS.**

Macaroni salad with nutmeg

Salade “macaronade” à la noix de muscade

SERVES 2 TO 4	PREPARATION: 30 minutes COOKING: 15 minutes REFRIGERATION: 4 hours

- ¾ pound (300 g) penne (fat short macaroni)
- 3 garlic cloves
- 3 ripe tomatoes
- 1 bunch of flat parsley
- 1 nutmeg
- 1 ball of mozzarella or ¼ pound (100 g) of feta
- 6 tablespoons (10 cl) olive oil
- 1 tablespoon sherry vinegar
- Fine salt, coarse salt

Cook the penne al dente (so the center is still firm) in a large pan of water seasoned with coarse salt, according to the time on the package. Refresh under cold water and drain well.

Peel the garlic and cut in half. In a salad bowl mix the penne, garlic, and olive oil. Cover and refrigerate for 4 hours.

Plunge the tomatoes in boiling water for 15 seconds, refresh under cold water, and peel. Cut them in quarters. Cut the mozzarella into dice. Chop the flat parsley. Take the salad bowl from the refrigerator, remove the garlic, and add the tomatoes, vinegar, and parsley. Sprinkle with 3 or 4 good gratings of nutmeg. Add salt and mix gently. Serve with the nutmeg and its grater so that each person can add seasoning to his or her taste. →

CHEF'S COMMENTS: Nutmeg adds an original touch to the well-known flavors of garlic and olive oil. This salad, which can be prepared in advance, can serve as a first course or a main course for a light summer dinner.

Find a good-quality sheep, goat, or water buffalo mozzarella or feta in a cheese or gourmet shop. Avoid the tasteless rubber too often sold by supermarkets for pizza.—**TRANS.**

3 Warm Starters

White meat turkey salad with vanilla oil
Salade de blanc de dinde à l'huile vanillée

SERVES 4 | PREPARATION: 15 minutes
COOKING: 3 minutes

1 uncooked turkey breast very finely sliced (allow about 2 ounces [60 g] per person)
½ pound (200 g) of lamb's lettuce (mâche), red butterhead (rougette), or another soft lettuce
Juice of ½ lemon
1 vanilla bean
6 tablespoons (10 cl) peanut oil
Fine salt

With a sharp knife, split the vanilla bean lengthwise. Scrape to remove the seeds. Mix the seeds with the oil and set aside.

Wash the lamb's lettuce three times, removing the stems. Dry it and put it in the salad bowl.

In a nonstick pan, heat the vanilla oil gently. Salt the slices of turkey, cook them in the oil for 10 seconds on each side, without coloring. Set aside.

Season the mâche with 3 tablespoons of vanilla oil, lemon juice, and a little salt. Put the salad on plates and add the turkey slices on top. Serve immediately.

CHEF'S COMMENTS: Vanilla is a forgotten spice for savory dishes. Here is a recipe that will flatter your palate! You must slice the turkey as finely as possible—as finely as cigarette paper.

While flavored oils are now available in gourmet shops, they often have strange tastes and the oils can be poor. Make your own. If you cannot cut the turkey so finely, use more per person and cook slightly longer. Vanilla oil could also be added to white or red beans.—**TRANS.**

Pumpkin flan with black sesame seeds and preserved gizzards

Flan de potimarron au sésame noir et aux gésiers confits

SERVES 4	PREPARATION: 15 minutes COOKING: 45 minutes

- 8 preserved gizzards
- 1½ pounds (600 g) pumpkin, peeled and cleaned
- 2 eggs
- 6 tablespoons (10 cl) whipping (heavy) cream
- 6 tablespoons (10 cl) milk
- 4 tablespoons toasted sesame oil
- 1 tablespoon black sesame seeds
- 1 bunch chives
- Salt, pepper

Cut the pumpkin in 1-inch (2 cm) pieces and cook for 15 minutes in a microwave oven (or cook in a moderate oven until tender).

Drain the gizzards, and dry on a paper towel. Cut them into quarters and place in four small ovenproof dishes.

Preheat the oven to 200°F (100°C).

When the pumpkin is cooked, blend it with the sesame oil, eggs, milk, cream, and salt and pepper for 1 minute. Add to the gizzards, put the dishes in a bain-marie, add very hot water, and cover. Cook in the oven for 30 minutes.

When the flans are cooked and removed from the oven, sprinkle with finely chopped chives and black sesame seeds. Serve warm.

CHEF'S COMMENTS: France and Japan meet in this dish. In Japan sesame is used a great deal; its subtle taste is found in many dishes. I find it hard to resist sticking a wet finger in sesame seeds, to crunch a few with delight. Toasted sesame oil, darker in color than raw sesame oil, is found in Chinese and Japanese dishes (whereas raw sesame oil is more appreciated by Indians).

Note the toasted sesame oil. It really is better for many dishes. The gizzards (either chicken or duck) are common in France, but they could be replaced by some dark meat, such as duck.—**TRANS.**

Lamb kidney salad with mixed spices
Salade tiède de rognons d'agneau en mendiant d'épices

SERVES 4

PREPARATION: 15 minutes
COOKING: 5 minutes

4 lamb kidneys, cut in two, with the nerves removed
¼ cup (2 oz, 50 g) corn
Red chicory or radiccio leaves (about 2 ounces)
½ cup (2 oz, 50 g) walnuts
4 dried apricots
10 fenugreek seeds
10 mustard seeds
10 coriander seeds
Pinch of curry powder
1 tablespoon balsamic vinegar
3 tablespoons walnut oil
1 tablespoon peanut oil
Salt, pepper

Mix together the vinegar, walnut oil, curry, and a little salt. Set aside.

Cover the walnuts and the spice seeds with water and boil for 2 minutes. Drain in a sieve.

Cut the apricots into small dice. Wash the lettuce. Drain the corn. Mix the spices and nuts with the corn and apricots.

Heat the peanut oil, salt the kidneys, and cook for 2 minutes on each side. Place in a dish to drain off their juice. Throw out the peanut oil, and in the same pan gently heat the mixture of corn, apricots, nuts, and spices.

Put the kidneys on the lettuce, sprinkle with the corn mixture, and add the vinaigrette.

CHEF'S COMMENTS: This warm salad resembles street food in China, where the ingredients are cooked on a hot fire in a wok and served immediately. The quality of the ingredients is heightened, and the spices add a touch of sauciness.

Canned corn is fine here, but fresh corn could be used for better taste.—**TRANS.**

Eggplant stuffed with feta, hazelnuts, and lemongrass

Aubergines à la feta, aux noisettes, et à la citronnelle

SERVES 4	PREPARATION: 30 minutes COOKING: 10 minutes

2 eggplants
Juice of 1 lemon
1 stalk of lemongrass
½ pound (250 g) Greek feta
½ cup (2 oz, 50 g) whole hazelnuts
6 tablespoons (10 cl) hazelnut oil
6 tablespoons (10 cl) olive oil
Salt, mignonnette pepper (long pepper)

Crush the hazelnuts with a knife, and toast them without oil in a frying pan. Set aside.

Mix the hazelnut oil and lemon juice, add about an inch of the bulb of the lemongrass, finely chopped. Wash and trim the eggplants, cutting them lengthwise into ½-inch (1 cm) slices (4 slices for each eggplant). Salt them.

In a large frying pan, heat half the olive oil and add the eggplant. Brown on one side, add a small glass of water, and cover the pan. When the water is completely evaporated, turn over the eggplant and let it brown. Repeat with the rest of the eggplant slices. Put 2 slices on each plate.

Crumble bits of feta on the warm eggplants and cover

with the vinaigrette. Add the mignonnette pepper and toasted hazelnuts.

CHEF'S COMMENTS: Here lemongrass is used like a shallot. It goes perfectly with feta.

The long pepper is a variety of black pepper, which could replace it.—**TRANS.**

Green asparagus with toasted spices
Asperges vertes au café d'épices

SERVES 4	PREPARATION: 30 minutes COOKING: 10 minutes

- 2 pounds (800 g) green asparagus
- Juice of 1 lime
- ¼ teaspoon coriander seeds
- ¼ teaspoon Szechuan pepper
- ¼ teaspoon cumin seeds
- ¼ teaspoon mustard seeds
- ¾ cup (20 cl) whipping (heavy) cream
- 1 tablespoon coarse salt
- Fine salt, freshly ground pepper

Peel the asparagus carefully with a peeler, starting at the head, taking care not to break them.

Heat the spices gently in a dry pan until they brown slightly, then grind in a blender or food processor for 10 seconds.

In a saucepan, boil the cream with the spices until the cream is reduced (about 2 minutes), then add the lime juice, fine salt, and pepper. Pour through a fine sieve.

Bring a large pan of water to boil, and season with coarse salt. Add the asparagus and cook for 5 minutes. Drain, then cut in 1½-inch (3 cm) pieces lengthwise. Serve covered with the cream sauce.

CHEF'S COMMENTS: When you are toasting and blending the spices, your kitchen will be full of delicious odors that will stay in your memory. You will be sure to make this again. A rare experience for the cook: the taste and the odor combine magnificently.

A trick to peeling asparagus is to hold the heads *up* away from you. The stalks are less likely to break this way.—**TRANS.**

Curried shrimp and sweet potatoes
Crevettes et patates douces au cari

SERVES 4

PREPARATION: 15 minutes
COOKING: 5 minutes

1 pound (400 g) cooked and shelled shrimp
1¼ pounds (500 g) sweet potatoes
¼ teaspoon curry powder
2 tablespoons balsamic vinegar
5 tablespoons peanut oil
5 tablespoons olive oil
1 bunch cilantro
Fine salt

Peel and wash the sweet potatoes. Cut in ⅛-inch (3 mm) rounds. Heat the peanut oil in a nonstick pan, and add the potato rounds so that all are touching the bottom of the pan. If your pan is small, do this in several batches. Cook for 3 minutes on each side, then drain on paper towels.

Mix together the vinegar, olive oil, curry powder, and a little salt.

Put the potato rounds in a rosette pattern on 4 plates. Warm the shrimp in the pan you used for the potatoes, then put them in the center of the pattern and add the vinaigrette. Sprinkle with cilantro.

CHEF'S COMMENTS: The sweet potato is rarely used in everyday cooking, so it can be surprising. Its slightly sweet taste blends with simple and sophisticated ingredients. It is marvelous with spices. There are several varieties: with white flesh, yellow flesh, orange flesh. The orange type with a slightly violet skin is the softest and sweetest. The sweet potato (*Ipomoea batatas*) does not belong to the potato family, but rather to the family of morning glories!

Sweet potatoes, particularly the orange variety, are recommended for their nutritional value. They are more common in the United States than in France. Do not refrigerate them. We always save shrimp, crawfish, and lobster shells to make a soup or sauce.—**TRANS.**

Wild mushroom mousse with saffron
Mousse de trompettes-des-morts au safran

SERVES 4	PREPARATION: 20 minutes COOKING: 15 minutes

1¼ pounds (500 g) wild mushrooms (*trompettes-des-morts*)
¾ pound (300 g) mushrooms (*champignons de Paris*)
1 shallot, finely chopped
½ garlic clove, grated
Pinch of saffron
½ cup (6 oz, 150 g) crème fraîche
2 tablespoons (1 oz, 30 g) butter
1 bunch of chervil
Fine salt

Cut the bottom off the mushrooms and the wild mushrooms and wash them thoroughly, changing the water three times. Dry them and cut the domestic mushrooms in thin slices. Slice the wild mushrooms lengthwise. Set aside.

Melt half the butter in a 12-inch (30 cm) frying pan, and cook the shallot for 1 minute without browning. Add the mushrooms, saving about a quarter of the wild mushrooms for later. Cover the pan for 1 minute, then let the moisture evaporate. Add the heavy cream, the garlic, and the saffron. Cook for 5 minutes, add salt, then blend this mixture to a fine paste. Heat the remaining butter, and sauté the remaining wild mushrooms until they are crispy. Put the puree on 4 plates, add the wild mushrooms, and decorate with sprigs of chervil.

CHEF'S COMMENTS: Flavors of the woods and the elegance of saffron make a real treat for the taste buds. You can replace *trompettes-des-morts* with any other wild mushrooms. ¼ teaspoon turmeric and ¼ teaspoon curry could replace the saffron.

Several different wild mushrooms are always available in Paris. In the United States you might need to settle for contrasting white and brown mushrooms.—**TRANS.**

Spiced white bean and wild mushroom salad
Salade épicée de haricots tarbais, champignons sauvages

SERVES 4

PREPARATION: 20 minutes
COOKING: 45 minutes
SOAKING: 12 hours

- ½ pound (200 g) white beans, soaked overnight
- 1 pound (400 g) wild mushrooms
- 1 shallot
- 1 onion
- 1 carrot
- 1 stalk celery
- ½ teaspoon coriander seeds
- ½ teaspoon sumac (or paprika)
- ½ teaspoon powdered coriander
- 2 tablespoons walnut oil
- 1 tablespoon sherry vinegar
- ½ teaspoon Meaux mustard
- 2 tablespoons (¾ oz, 20 g) butter
- Salt, freshly ground pepper

Peel the onion and cut it in quarters. Peel and finely chop the shallot. Wash and peel the carrot and celery. Trim and quickly wash the mushrooms.

Sweat the mushrooms for 2 minutes in a covered pan on medium heat. Drain in a sieve, saving the juice.

Rinse and drain the beans. Put them in a pan with the mushroom juice, coriander seeds, carrot, onion, and celery. Cover with water and cook 45 minutes, or until the beans are tender.

Mix the walnut oil, powdered spices, mustard, and vinegar. Add salt.

In a frying pan, heat the butter and cook the mushrooms with the shallot. Season.

Drain the beans and discard the carrot, onion, and celery. Put the beans in a serving bowl, add the vinaigrette, mix, then cover the dish with the mushrooms.

CHEF'S COMMENTS: The acidity of the sumac and coriander make this autumn dish a festival of tastes.

Simmer white beans (do not boil), as they can become mushy. Fresh white beans are best. If you have no time to soak them overnight, pour boiling water over the beans and let them sit for an hour. Then drain, and start the recipe.—**TRANS.**

Potatoes stuffed with oysters, with curry sauce
Pommes de terre farcies aux huîtres, sauce cari

SERVES 4	PREPARATION: 20 minutes COOKING: 20 minutes

16 large oysters (in France, Marennes no. 1)
16 rather small new potatoes
(Belle de Fontenay or Charlotte if possible)
2 shallots, peeled and chopped
½ teaspoon curry powder
3 tablespoons (5 cl) dry white wine
1½ cups (40 cl) crème fraîche
Chervil or parsley, chopped
Fine salt, coarse salt, freshly ground white pepper

Put the shallots in a pan with the wine and curry powder, and reduce until almost dry. Set aside.

Open the oysters, detach them from their shells, and filter the juice through a sieve. Keep the oysters cool, and save the juice. Cook the potatoes in their skins in lightly salted water until tender.

Add the oyster juice to the curry and wine reduction and reduce by half over medium heat. Add the crème fraîche, simmer for about 6 minutes, until the sauce thickens. Season to taste, but do so carefully as the oyster juice is very salty, so taste before adding salt. Cut the potatoes in half, horizontally, at ⅔ of their height, then hollow them with a small spoon. Cut a small slice on the bottom so the potato will be stable. Put 4 potatoes on each plate.

Briefly heat the oysters with the remaining juice. Put 1 oyster in each potato and cover with the sauce. Serve immediately, with chervil or flat parsley.

CHEF'S COMMENTS: Here is a way of combining the iodine taste of the oysters with the spicy flavor of curry. As both of these flavors are strong, in this recipe the potatoes add a tempering touch. Your meal will start with panache.

If using those packaged or shelled fresh oysters found in American markets, be certain to sieve out the bits of shell.—**TRANS.**

Chanterelle mushroom cakes with kaffir lime leaves
Gâteau de girolles aux feuilles de limettier

SERVES 4	PREPARATION: 25 minutes COOKING: 40 minutes

1½ pounds (600 g) chanterelle mushrooms
3 eggs
Juice of 1 lemon
½ garlic clove, grated
1 small bunch of chives
6 kaffir lime leaves
(or 1 stalk of lemongrass; if neither is available, substitute 1 tablespoon curry powder)
¾ cup (8 oz, 200 g) crème fraîche
2 tablespoons walnut oil
1 tablespoon sherry vinegar
Salt, freshly ground pepper

Preheat the oven to 350°F (180°C).

Cut the lime leaves in half (or split the stalk of lemongrass). Clean and wash the chanterelles. Sweat them in a covered pan over low heat. When their moisture is almost completely evaporated, add the crème fraîche, garlic, and lime leaves (or lemongrass). Reduce for 10 minutes. Season with salt and pepper. Remove the lime leaves.

Put the chanterelles in a blender, add the lemon juice, and blend to a smooth puree. Break the eggs and add to the blender. Blend for another 10 seconds. Put this mixture in small oven molds (the size of a crème caramel mold) and bake for 30 minutes.

Prepare a vinaigrette with the walnut oil and sherry vinegar. Chop the chives. Put the vinaigrette and chives on the flans and serve immediately.

CHEF'S COMMENTS: Kaffir lime leaves or lemongrass add an astonishing fresh flavor. These cakes are a fine first course during the mushroom season.

If you cannot get chanterelles, use a brown mushroom.—**TRANS.**

Cooked foie gras of duck with cinnamon
Foie gras de canard poêlé à la cannelle

SERVES 4	PREPARATION: 25 minutes SOAKING: 12 hours COOKING: about 1 hour

8 slices of duck foie gras (liver) about ½ inch (1 cm) thick (tell the butcher you are going to brown the foie gras)
4 tablespoons (2 oz, 50 g) chickpeas
Juice of ½ lemon
2 pinches of powdered cinnamon
1 tablespoon honey
Salt, freshly ground white pepper

Soak the chickpeas in cold water overnight. The next day, rinse and drain them, cover with lightly salted water, bring to a boil, and cook until tender (about 1 hour), then drain.

Season the foie gras slices with salt and pepper. Keep them cold.

Put the chickpeas in a frying pan with honey and cinnamon, and cook over medium heat until caramelized. Then add 6 tablespoons (10 cl) water and the lemon juice. Reduce by half. Check the seasoning. Keep warm.

Heat a dry frying pan. When it is hot, lower the heat and brown the slices of foie gras for 1 minute on each side. Put them on 4 plates and add the chickpea sauce. Serve immediately.

CHEF'S COMMENTS: This is a recipe for holidays. Be careful not to use too much cinnamon, so that it surprises without being aggressive.

If you cannot find foie gras of duck, you might try chicken livers.—**TRANS.**

Scallops in soy sauce butter
Coquilles Saint-Jacques au beurre de soja

SERVES 4 | PREPARATION: 15 minutes
COOKING: 1 minute

12 fresh scallops
Juice of ½ lemon
4 tablespoons (2 oz, 50 g) cold butter
3 tablespoons crème fraîche
4 tablespoons soy sauce
1½ tablespoons olive oil
Salt, freshly ground pepper

Cut each scallop horizontally into 2 slices. Salt them very lightly and keep cold.

In a saucepan, reduce the soy sauce by half, add the crème fraîche, and reduce to thicken. Off the heat, add the cold butter with a whisk, then a few drops of lemon juice. Reheat but don't boil.

In a nonstick pan, heat the olive oil. Cook the scallops for 10 seconds on each side. Drain on a paper towel.

Cover the scallops with the sauce. Add pepper.

CHEF'S COMMENTS: In this recipe, soy sauce is the spice. Its caramelized flavor covers the tender scallops, and its taste could be mistaken for truffle butter. If you find the taste too strong, add another tablespoon of butter.

The scallops must be cooked very quickly to avoid hardening. If your pan is not large enough, cook in two batches. This recipe is simple and delicious.—**TRANS.**

Lobster stew with green peas and cinnamon
Cassolette de homard aux petits pois et à la cannelle

SERVES 2 | PREPARATION: 45 minutes
COOKING: 20 minutes

1 live lobster, 1 to 1½ pounds (500 to 600 g)
½ pound (200 g) young green peas, shelled
Juice of ½ lemon
Pinch of powdered cinnamon
4 tablespoons (2 oz, 50 g) butter
6 tablespoons (10 cl) dry white wine
Pinch of brown sugar
1 tablespoon olive oil
Salt, freshly ground pepper

Put the lobster in cold salted water, bring to simmer, cook 5 minutes. Drain and keep in a sieve.

Cook the peas in salted boiling water for 8 minutes. Plunge when cooked into cold water. Drain.

Take the shell off the lobster. Cut the tail in rounds about ½ inch (1 cm) thick. Keep the head for decoration.

Crush the carcass. Put in a pan with the cinnamon, white wine, and 6 tablespoons (10 cl) water. Reduce by half. Strain through a fine sieve into a small pan, add and blend the butter in small dice, sugar, lemon juice, and salt. Taste and adjust the seasoning.

Heat the olive oil in a nonstick pan. Cook the rounds of lobster for 15 seconds, add the peas. Heat for 30 seconds, stirring gently. Put onto plates and cover with the sauce. Decorate with the lobster head cut in two. →

CHEF'S COMMENTS: For grand occasions, especially in lobster season. Again, be careful not to use too much cinnamon, which must not overwhelm the dish.

This could be made with rock lobster tails or large shrimp. We always brown the shells rapidly to improve the flavor before making a sauce (or soup). This is one of those recipes that the home cook might want to start in advance, unless you are used to making reductions.—**TRANS.**

Scallops with lemongrass
Coquilles Saint-Jacques à la nage de citronnelle

SERVES 2 | PREPARATION: 20 minutes
COOKING: 45 minutes

6 sea scallops
Bones of white fish (sole or turbot, preferably)
1 onion, peeled
1 sprig thyme
1 bay leaf
Juice of ½ lemon
1 stalk lemongrass
1 slice fresh ginger
Pinch of paprika
4 kaffir lime leaves (or the zest of ½ lime)
4 tablespoons (2 oz, 50 g) butter
Salt, freshly ground pepper

Cut each scallop horizontally into two slices. Season with salt and pepper on both sides.

Rinse the bones in cold water. Put them in a small pan with the onion cut in thin slices, thyme, and bay leaf. Add 1 quart (1 liter) water. Cook for 20 minutes at high heat, then filter the stock through a fine sieve. You should have about 1 pint (50 cl).

Put the stock, ginger, kaffir lime leaves, and lemongrass in a blender and process for 15 seconds. Bring the stock back to a boil and filter into a frying pan. Reduce to about ¾ cup (20 cl).

Clean the blender and add the cold butter cut in small pieces. Add the boiling stock, blending at high speed until the butter →

forms an emulsion. Add the lemon juice and salt. Put this sauce into a frying pan and add the scallop slices. Let simmer for 5 seconds. Check the seasoning. Serve in warm dishes, and sprinkle with paprika.

CHEF'S COMMENTS: This is a variation of the Thai soup tom yam kum, with the addition of the butter. The kaffir lime leaves and lemongrass are the two essential flavors of this soup. The subtlety and delicacy of the lemongrass and its exotic freshness possess a real magic.

Do not overcook fish bones, as the broth becomes bitter. And yes, you can cheat with a fish soup cube, but add salt carefully.—**TRANS.**

Cockles with Espelette pepper
Poêlée de coques au piment d'Espelette

SERVES 4	PREPARATION: 35 minutes COOKING: 10 minutes

3¼ pounds (1.5 kg) cockles
1 onion
1 stalk lemongrass
½ teaspoon powdered Espelette pepper (or a powdered dried pepper)
½ teaspoon ras el-hanout
½ teaspoon freshly ground black pepper
3 tablespoons (5 cl) olive oil
½ teaspoon sugar
1 garlic clove
coarse salt

Peel and chop the onion. Chop finely the bulb of the lemongrass. Wash the cockles in three changes of water, soaking them 10 minutes each time.

In a large pan, heat the olive oil with the onion and lemongrass. Cook gently for 1 minute. Add the sugar and the spices (except the pepper) and cook for 1 minute. Peel and grate the garlic and add. Cook 1 minute.

Add the cockles, ¾ cup (20 cl) water, and a pinch of coarse salt. Bring to a boil and cook, stirring, for 1 minute. Sprinkle with the Espelette and serve immediately. →

CHEF'S COMMENTS: This is a quick preparation, which cockles require. The Espelette pepper, added at the last minute, gives the iodine of the cockles a lively flavor.

Make certain the sand is washed out of the cockles. Espelette can be replaced by a good Spanish paprika.—**TRANS.**

4 Soups

Cold avocado and shrimp soup with sesame seeds
Crème froide d'avocat au sésame et aux crevettes

SERVES 6

PREPARATION: 25 minutes
COOKING: 35 minutes
REFRIGERATION: at least 2 hours

¾ pound (300 g) chicken wings
½ pound (200 g) large shrimp, shelled
2 ripe avocados
Juice of 1 lemon
1 carrot
1 onion
1 stalk celery
1 leek
¾ cup (20 cl) whipping (heavy) cream
2 tablespoons (1 oz, 25 g) butter
4 tablespoons (1 oz, 25 g) flour
1 tablespoon toasted sesame seeds

Peel and wash the carrot, onion, celery, and leek. Cut the chicken wings into small pieces. Put all these ingredients in a large pot with 3 quarts (3 liters) of water and boil at high heat for 30 minutes until 1 quart remains.

In another pan, melt the butter and add the flour, stirring together with a whisk. Pour the stock over the butter and flour roux in three batches. Add the cream and whisk until the sauce thickens. Cool, then refrigerate for at least 2 hours.

When the soup is cold, blend it with the pulp of the avocados and the lemon juice until smooth.

Cut the shrimp in rounds and put into the soup bowls. Cover with the avocado soup, then sprinkle the toasted sesame seeds.

CHEF'S COMMENTS: A creamy, refreshing summer soup. The toasted sesame recalls the seasonings the Japanese use in some of their soups.

Simple and good, but you need to start hours in advance to allow time for the reduction and cooling. The actual putting together of the dish is rapid.—**TRANS.**

Tomato and turmeric soup
Soupe de tomates au curcuma

SERVES 4 | PREPARATION: 20 minutes
COOKING: 10 minutes

¾ cup (6 oz, 150 g) grated coconut
6 ripe tomatoes (olivettes, if possible)
1 onion, chopped
Juice of ½ lime
1 small garlic clove
1 fresh bird pepper, or Vietnamese pepper (optional)
1 piece of ginger the size of a garlic clove, grated
½ teaspoon turmeric
½ teaspoon powdered coriander
1 tablespoon peanut oil
Salt, freshly ground white pepper

In a blender add 2 cups (50 cl) boiling water to the grated coconut. Blend for 2 minutes. Put through a fine sieve, pressing to extract all the coconut milk.

Wash the tomatoes, remove the stems, and cut each into 6 pieces. Remove the seeds from the pepper and chop finely. Grate the ginger and the garlic.

Heat the oil in a saucepan, add the onion, ginger, pepper, garlic and powdered spices. Cook for 1 minute on low heat. Add the coconut milk, simmer for 5 minutes. Then add the tomatoes and lime juice and cook for 2 minutes. Season with salt and pepper.

Put the pieces of tomato in the soup plates then gently cover with the soup. Serve.

CHEF'S COMMENTS: This soup, inspired by India, can be eaten warm or cold and keeps well in the refrigerator. If you want more flavor, add cilantro before serving.

Bird pepper is similar to cayenne pepper or Thai chili pepper. One pepper is the equivalent of ⅛ teaspoon of ground pepper. Olivette tomatoes are shaped like large olives or large Roma tomatoes (which would be a good substitute).—**TRANS.**

Cold cucumber and cilantro soup
Soupe froide de concombre à la coriandre

SERVES 4

PREPARATION: 30 minutes
COOKING: 12 minutes
REFRIGERATION: 4 hours

- 2 cucumbers
- 1 large onion, finely chopped
- ½ garlic clove, grated
- 40 cilantro leaves
- 10 fresh mint leaves
- 2 cups (50 cl) chicken stock
- 6 tablespoons thick crème fraîche
- 2 tablespoons sherry vinegar
- 2 tablespoons olive oil
- Salt, freshly ground pepper

Peel the cucumbers and cut in two lengthwise. Remove the seeds with a spoon and cut in thin slices.

Heat the oil in a pan over low heat. Add the onion and garlic, and cook for a minute without browning. Add the cucumbers and mix with a wooden spoon. Add the chicken stock and crème fraîche. Cook for 10 minutes. Add salt and pepper.

Put half of the mixture in a blender. Blend for a minute with half of the mint, half of the coriander, and 1 tablespoon of the vinegar. Repeat for the other half. Then put all the mixture through a fine sieve. Refrigerate for at least 4 hours. Beat the soup before serving and sprinkle with more coriander.

CHEF'S COMMENTS: This is a light and refreshing starter. The cilantro is a delight for the senses.

Fresh cilantro is called for here, but you could substitute a good green dried mint. A good tip for soups is to blend in the fresh herbs after cooking or in the last minute of cooking. Variations on gazpacho, slightly cooked rather than raw, are popular now in France; they are smoother, hence the cream.

At his restaurant, Delacourcelle has served this soup with a quenelle of crabmeat.—**TRANS.**

Pumpkin and lemongrass soup
Soupe de potimarron à la citronnelle

SERVES 4

PREPARATION: 30 minutes
COOKING: 40 minutes

12 ounces (300 g) chicken wings
2¼ pounds (1 kg) pumpkin
Juice of ½ lemon
1 stalk celery
1 carrot
1 onion
1 leek
2 stalks of lemongrass, crushed
¾ cup (20 cl) whipping (heavy) cream
2 tablespoons (1 oz, 25 g) butter
4 tablespoons (1 oz, 25 g) flour
1 tablespoon hazelnut oil
Fine salt

Peel and wash the celery, carrot, onion, and leek. Cut them into rounds. Cut the chicken wings into small pieces and add to a large pot with the vegetables and lemongrass. Cover with 3 quarts (3 liters) of water, bring to boil, and cook for 30 minutes until 1 quart of liquid is left.

Peel the pumpkin and remove the center and seeds. Cut the pulp into 1-inch (2 cm) dice, and steam or cook for 10 minutes in the microwave.

In another large pan, melt the butter, add the flour, and whisk together. Add the stock through a sieve in 3 batches, taking care to mix well after each batch of liquid. Add the cream and boil for 5 minutes.

In a blender, puree the pumpkin and add the stock until smooth. Check the seasoning and add the lemon juice and hazelnut oil.

CHEF'S COMMENTS: This is a mixture of France and Asia, with hazelnut oil and lemongrass. They complement each other subtly: freshness, flavors, smoothness—everything is here. Even people suspicious of pumpkin will be impressed.

As usual, the home cook might want to substitute a bouillon cube for the excellent chicken stock that French restaurants always seem to have on boil.—**TRANS.**

Lemon soup with saffron
Soupe de citron confit au safran

SERVES 4	PREPARATION: 20 minutes COOKING: 40 minutes

- ¾ pound (300 g) chicken wings
- 1 stalk celery
- 1 carrot
- 1 leek
- 1 onion
- 1 untreated lemon
- ½ teaspoon powdered saffron or a pinch of saffron pistils
- ¾ cup (20 cl) whipping (heavy) cream
- 2 tablespoons (1 oz, 25 g) butter
- 4 tablespoons (1 oz, 25 g) flour
- Salt, freshly ground pepper

Peel and wash the celery, carrot, leek, and onion. Cut the chicken wings into small pieces and add to a pot with the vegetables. Cover with 3 quarts (3 liters) of water and boil for 30 minutes at high heat until 1 quart of stock remains.

In another pan, cover the lemon with water, bring to a boil, and cook for 5 minutes. Throw out the water and repeat this operation 3 more times. Remove the lemon from the pan and cut into 2 pieces.

In a third pan, melt the butter, add the flour and the saffron, whisking together. Add the stock in 4 batches, through a sieve, mixing well with each batch of liquid. Add the cream and boil for 5 minutes.

In a blender, puree half the lemon (the other half can be frozen and saved for another time) and the stock (the soup should come halfway up the blender bowl). Pour soup through a fine sieve. Check the seasoning.

CHEF'S COMMENTS: This soup, which I thought of as a hot soup, can also be served cold. The addition of a preserved lemon adds a Mediterranean accent, and the saffron provides an accent of the Near East. In the summer I add small dice of cooked artichoke hearts.

We once used half a preserved lemon from a Middle Eastern shop, which made a different and interesting soup.—**TRANS.**

Caribbean mussel soup with almonds
Soupe de moules aux amandes et au colombo

SERVES 4	PREPARATION: 15 minutes COOKING: 10 to 15 minutes

- 1 quart (1 liter, about 1 pound) mussels
- ¼ pound (100 g) potatoes (Belle de Fontenay or Charlotte if possible) or new potatoes, cut into ½-inch (1 cm) dice
- 1 onion, chopped
- 2 leeks, finely chopped
- 1 sprig thyme
- 1 bay leaf
- ½ teaspoon powdered Colombo (or Indian curry)
- 1 teaspoon crushed almonds
- 6 tablespoons (10 cl) crème fraîche
- 2 tablespoons (1 oz, 20 g) butter
- 2 tablespoons flour
- ¾ cup (20 cl) dry white wine

Scrape and wash the mussels in several changes of water. Submerge the potatoes in cold water to keep them fresh.

In a large pan, melt the butter for 2 minutes with the onion and leeks. Add the Colombo and cook for 1 minute. Add the flour and cook another minute, mixing continually with a wooden spoon. Set aside.

In another pan, bring the white wine to boil with 2 cups (50 cl) water and the thyme and bay leaf. Add the mussels for 2 minutes, until they open. Filter the liquid through a fine sieve into the first pan, whisking energetically. Add the crème fraîche and the potatoes and cook for 5 minutes or until the potatoes are cooked.

Shell the mussels and put into 4 soup bowls.

Lightly brown the almonds in a dry pan. Pour the boiling soup on the mussels, and sprinkle each plate with the almonds. Serve hot.

CHEF'S COMMENTS: Colombo is a Caribbean version of curry. The combination of spices is different but always very flavorful and spicy. Pay attention to the quantity of spice.

When cleaning mussels it is essential to pull off the "beard," the algae that it uses to hold on to rocks. Do not prepare mussels too far in advance of cooking, as they die quickly.—**TRANS.**

Clam broth with kaffir lime leaves
Bouillon de palourdes aux feuilles de limettier

SERVES 4	PREPARATION: 25 minutes COOKING: 10 minutes SOAKING: 1 hour

2¼ pounds (1 kg) clams
2 tomatoes, not too ripe
Juice of ½ lime
2 shallots, peeled
½ tablespoon (⅓ oz, 10 g) fresh ginger, peeled
2 kaffir lime leaves (or 3 inches of untreated lime skin)
1 stalk lemongrass
½ cup (4 oz, 100 g) butter
¾ cup (20 cl) dry white wine
A few sprigs cilantro
Salt, freshly ground pepper

Soak the clams for 1 hour in fresh water. Carefully lift them out of the water, leaving the sand in the bottom of the pan. Rinse in three or four changes of water and set aside in a large pan.

Rinse the kaffir lime leaves and the bulb of the lemongrass. Puree the shallots, ginger, kaffir lime leaves, and lemongrass in a blender to create a paste.

In a pan, melt about 2 tablespoons of butter, add the paste, and cook for 1 minute over low heat. Add the wine and 1 cup (30 cl) water, and boil for 5 minutes. Pour this broth through a fine sieve over the clams. Cover the pan and bring to a boil, stirring with a wooden spoon. Cook, covered, for 2 minutes. Put the broth into another pan, keeping the clams separate. Bring the broth to boil, add the lime juice, and whisk in the rest of the butter in small pieces.

Peel the tomatoes after plunging them in boiling water for a few seconds. Cut them into ½-inch (1 cm) dice. Add them to the broth along with the cilantro, salt, and pepper.

Put the clams into soup bowls and add the hot broth.

CHEF'S COMMENTS: This soup alludes to tom yam kum, its light and flavorful Thai counterpart.

The butter and wine make this soup French. For a less creamy soup, eliminate or cut down on the amount of butter.—**TRANS.**

Curried cream of lentil soup

Crème de lentilles au cari

SERVES 4 TO 6

PREPARATION: 15 minutes
COOKING: 30 minutes

- ¼ pound (100 g) smoked bacon
- ½ pound (200 g) lentils, rinsed and drained
- 1 onion, finely chopped
- 1 stick cinnamon
- 1 clove
- 1 level tablespoon curry powder
- ¼ teaspoon powdered coriander
- ¾ cup (20 cl) crème fraîche
- ¾ cup (20 cl) milk
- 2 tablespoons (1 oz, 20 g) butter
- Salt

Cut the skin from the bacon and chop into small dice. In a large pan, heat the butter, and add the onion and bacon. Cook gently for 1 minute, stirring with a wooden spoon. Add the spices, mix well, then add the lentils. Cook for 1 minute, stirring. Add 1 quart (1 liter) water and cook for 30 minutes over low heat.

When the cooking is finished and the lentils have absorbed almost all the water, add the milk and the crème fraîche. Bring to a boil and salt to taste. Remove the cinnamon and clove.

In two batches, pour into a blender and puree for 30 seconds. Dilute the soup with a little milk if necessary and put it through a fine sieve to get rid of the skin on the lentils. Reheat and serve immediately.

CHEF'S COMMENTS: When I was in Asia I had several opportunities to eat Indian dal, which inspired this soup, adapted to European taste.

Those who don't like smoked bacon could use some chicken stock.—**TRANS.**

Chicken broth with Chinese spices
Bouillon simple de poule aux épices chinoises

SERVES 4 | PREPARATION: 25 minutes
COOKING: 20 minutes

- ½ pound (200 g) chicken breast, skin removed
- 2 to 3 hen or chicken carcasses or 1 pound (500 g) of chicken wings, cut into small pieces
- 1 leek
- 1 carrot
- 1 onion
- 1 lettuce
- 1 bay leaf
- 1 sprig thyme
- A few blades of chives
- 6 whole star anise
- 1 stick Chinese cinnamon (cassia)
- ½ bunch cilantro
- 4 tablespoons soy sauce
- ¼ pound (100 g) soybean sprouts (optional)

Peel and wash all the vegetables. Chop finely the carrot, leek, and onion. Cut the lettuce in strips and set aside.

Place the carcasses or chicken wings in a pot with all the vegetables (except the lettuce, chives, and cilantro), the star anise, cinnamon, bay leaf, and thyme. Cover with 4 quarts (4 liters) of water, bring to a boil, and skim the fat until the liquid is clear. Boil for 30 minutes until the broth is reduced by half.

During this time, cut the chicken breasts in very thin slices. Cut the chives with scissors. Prepare 4 soup bowls.

Add the chicken broth to another pan, bring to a boil, and add the chicken breast slices. Cook for 1 minute.

In each bowl, add the lettuce, 1 tablespoon soy sauce, and the chopped chives. Add the pieces of chicken and the fresh cilantro leaves (if you are using soybean sprouts, add these too). Into each bowl pour the boiling broth. You will want to adjust the seasoning at the table.

CHEF'S COMMENTS: In China this soup is served for breakfast. Here it can be prepared in advance, kept refrigerated and served impromptu—for example, to guests coming back late from a party.

This follows the basic principle for many oriental soups in which the hot broth is poured over raw salad ingredients, especially lettuce, soybeans, cucumber, radish slices, herbs, or thin slices of carrot.—**TRANS.**

5 Fish

Tuna with white sesame seed crust
Tranche de thon croûtée au sésame blond

SERVES 4	PREPARATION: 15 minutes COOKING: 5 minutes

4 fresh tuna steaks, about 1 inch (2.5 cm) thick
2 tablespoons olive oil
6 tablespoons white sesame seeds
1 pinch of coarse sel de Guérande
Fine salt

Pour the sesame seeds on a plate. Salt the tuna very lightly on both sides. Place the tuna steaks on the sesame seeds, and press well to make the seeds stick.

In a nonstick pan, heat the olive oil. Add the tuna, seed side down, and cook for 3 minutes over low heat. The seeds should turn golden but not burn. Turn the tuna over and cook for 2 minutes. The cooking time depends on the thickness of the steaks and your taste; watch carefully to make the tuna steaks just right.

Sprinkle a bit of coarse sel de Guérande on each steak and serve immediately.

CHEF'S COMMENTS: The contrast between the crunchiness of the sesame and the tenderness of the tuna is very subtle. You can make a more colorful dish by mixing white and black sesame seeds.

Tuna is a rich fish. Better to serve smaller than larger steaks. Many people prefer it when it is still raw inside. You could also use poppy seeds instead of sesame seeds.—**TRANS.**

Braised sea bass, orange peel, and cilantro
Bar à l'étouffée, écorce d'orange, et coriandre fraîche

SERVES 4 | PREPARATION: 20 minutes
COOKING: 5 minutes

Fillets of a 2½-pound (1.2 kg) bass, skin on
1 ripe tomato, seeds removed, diced
Juice of ½ lemon
1 orange
1 shallot, finely chopped
1 bunch of cilantro
1 tablespoon sesame seeds
3 tablespoons (5 cl) olive oil
½ teaspoon coarse sel de Guérande
Salt, freshly ground pepper

Peel the skin of the orange and cut it into small dice. Add the orange peel to a pan. Cover with 1 quart of water and bring to a boil. Pour over a fine sieve. Repeat this procedure two more times, then dry the orange peel on a paper towel. Juice half the orange.

In a dry frying pan, cook the sesame seeds until golden.

Put the orange peel, shallot, tomato, sesame seeds, and the juice of the lemon and orange in a saucepan. Add salt and pepper and most of the olive oil (save 1 tablespoon for the fish). Heat gently for 1 minute.

Heat the rest of the olive oil in a nonstick pan. Salt the fish fillets and put them skin-side down in the pan. Cook for 1 minute, then cover and braise for 3 more minutes. →

Put the fish in a serving dish, and cover with the sauce and a few grains of sel de Guérande and sprigs of cilantro.

CHEF'S COMMENTS: In Asia cilantro is used in many dishes, as parsley is in the West. Its fresh, subtle flavor transforms each dish into a taste treat.

Because of the influence of Latin American cuisine, cilantro is more common in the United States than in France. Orange and cilantro is an excellent combination, as is orange, cilantro, and ginger.—**TRANS.**

Cuttlefish with green peppercorns
Blancs de seiche au poivre vert

SERVES 4 | PREPARATION: 30 minutes
COOKING: 20 minutes

2 pounds (800 g) white flesh of cuttlefish, cut into 1½-inch (4 cm) squares
1 large shallot, chopped
1 clove garlic, unpeeled
1 red bell pepper, seeded and cut into ½-inch (1 cm) dice
1 tablespoon (⅓ oz, 10 g) green peppercorns
6 tablespoons (10 cl) dry white wine
6 tablespoons (10 cl) crème fraîche
2 tablespoons (3 cl) olive oil
Salt, freshly ground pepper

Heat half the olive oil and sweat the shallot, bell pepper, and unpeeled garlic for 10 minutes over low heat. Remove the garlic after cooking.

Season the cuttlefish with salt and pepper. Heat the rest of the oil in a frying pan. When the oil is hot, cook the cuttlefish 3 minutes on each side, then remove from the heat and discard the oil. In the same pan, reduce the white wine with the green peppercorns, scraping to get all the juices. When the wine is reduced to about 1 tablespoon, add the bell pepper and shallot. Cook for 3 minutes over low heat, then add the crème fraîche and boil for 1 minute. Season with salt and add the fish. Do not bring to a boil. Serve immediately. →

CHEF'S COMMENTS: Green peppercorns can be very strong, so be careful, but their flavor is unique. In Japan, for holidays, you can buy grilled cuttlefish on a stick, like a caramel apple. It's delicious.

Squid, octopus, and cuttlefish are basic to cooking in most of the world. The flesh is sweet if a little bland and is best spiced up a bit, especially with pepper.—**TRANS.**

Cod with lemongrass

Brandade de morue à la citronnelle

SERVES 4	PREPARATION: 30 minutes COOKING: 35 minutes

1½ pounds (600 g) fresh cod, bones and skin removed
1 pound (400 g) potatoes (Belle de Fontenay or Charlotte, if possible, or new potatoes)
2 cloves garlic, peeled and cut into two pieces each
1 stalk lemongrass
5 kaffir lime leaves (or, as a substitute, another stalk of lemongrass and the zest of ¼ lime)
2 cups (50 cl) milk
4 tablespoons (2 oz, 50 g) butter
3 tablespoons (5 cl) olive oil
Fine salt

Preheat the oven to 300°F (150°C).

Wash and brush the potatoes, cover them with lightly salted water in a pot, and cook for 20 minutes or until cooked through. Drain.

Put the cod in a pan with high sides, cover with milk, and add the kaffir lime leaves, the lemongrass, the garlic cloves, and a little salt. Simmer for 5 minutes. Remove the fish, reserving the cooking liquid, and crumble the flesh. Remove the lime leaves and lemongrass.

Peel the cooked potatoes and crush them, one by one, with a fork. Combine the cod and the potatoes with a fork.

Cut the lemongrass into small pieces and put it in a blender with lime leaves and the butter. Bring the liquid used for →

cooking the fish to a boil and add 6 tablespoons of it to the blender. Blend for 15 seconds, then pour through a sieve onto the fish. Mix. Taste and correct the seasoning.

Pour the mixture into an ovenproof dish and cover with olive oil. Heat for 15 minutes, then serve on a platter. You could also put the fish on individual plates and accompany it with a mixed salad.

CHEF'S COMMENTS: This is a fresh and original variation of the traditional *brandade*, an encounter between France and the flavors of Asia.

Versions of cod (more often salted cod) and potatoes are common around the world. Although delicious on their own, such dishes are usually spiced up or cooked with a spicy vegetable combination.—**TRANS.**

Sautéed hake with wasabi

Merlu poêlé au raifort japonais *wasabi*

SERVES 4 | PREPARATION: 20 minutes
COOKING: 10 minutes

- 4 hake steaks of about ½ pound (200 g) each
- 1 shallot, peeled and chopped
- ¼ teaspoon powdered wasabi
- 6 tablespoons (10 cl) fish stock (optional)
- 3 tablespoons (5 cl) dry white wine
- 6 tablespoons (10 cl) crème fraîche
- 4 tablespoons (2 oz, 50 g) butter
- 3 tablespoons (5 cl) olive oil
- Salt

Put the shallots, white wine, and fish stock (if you use it) in a pan and reduce until almost dry. Add the crème fraîche and the wasabi (slowly, tasting to be sure it is not too strong). Reduce again for 3 minutes, then whisk in the butter.

Heat the olive oil in a nonstick pan. Salt the hake steaks and fry them until golden, about 5 minutes on each side. Correct the seasoning if necessary. Put the fish on a serving dish and add the sauce. Serve immediately.

CHEF'S COMMENTS: You can find wasabi in Japanese and Chinese groceries. It is best to buy it in powdered form. You can dilute it with a little water to create a thick paste to accompany raw fish. Be careful, as wasabi is very strong. Don't lick the spoon.

Wasabi is found in almost all American supermarkets, where it is better known than in France. It makes an interesting substitution for mustard in sauces.—**TRANS.**

Sea trout with matcha

Minute de truite de mer au thé vert *matcha*

SERVES 4	PREPARATION: 25 minutes COOKING: 5 minutes

4 scallops of sea trout, about 7 ounces (180 g) each
Juice of ½ lemon
1 shallot, peeled and finely chopped
3 tablespoons (5 cl) dry white wine
¾ cup (20 cl) fish stock (optional)
1 tablespoon powdered Japanese green tea
6 tablespoons (10 cl) crème fraîche
4 tablespoons (2 oz, 50 g) butter
3 tablespoons (5 cl) olive oil
Salt, freshly ground pepper

Put the white wine, the fish stock (if you use it), and the shallot in a pan and reduce until almost dry. Add the crème fraîche and the powdered tea, and whisk for about 3 minutes while it reduces. Whisk in butter and lemon juice. Add salt and pepper.

Heat the olive oil in a nonstick pan. Salt and pepper the trout slices and brown quickly over high heat. Lower the heat and cook the fish without turning over the slices. You can control the cooking by turning the fish when the color has reached halfway up the pieces. Once the pieces have been turned, cook for 5 seconds and remove from the pan.

Place the trout on plates and cover with the sauce. Serve immediately.

CHEF'S COMMENTS: Green tea, matcha, reduced to fine powder, is used in Japan for the tea ceremony and also for desserts (ices and sweet gelatin desserts). Its sharp tannin taste goes well with a fatty fish. This is a spice in its own right.

Half-cooked fish is excellent. The trick is to cook it thoroughly on one side, then hardly at all on the other side, as here. In another method, a thick fish fillet is roasted at a very low temperature for 20 to 25 minutes.—**TRANS.**

Roasted John Dory with kaffir lime leaves

Saint-pierre rôti aux feuilles de limettier

SERVES 4	PREPARATION: 15 minutes COOKING: 20 minutes

1 John Dory of 2½ to 3 pounds (1.2 to 1.5 kg), cleaned and whole
20 kaffir lime leaves
3 tablespoons (5 cl) olive oil
Fine salt, coarse sel de Guérande, freshly ground pepper

Preheat the oven to 350°F (180°C).

Salt and pepper the fish on all sides, and put 5 kaffir lime leaves in the cavity. Make small incisions in the fish and put lime leaves under the skin.

In an ovenproof pan large enough to hold the fish, heat the olive oil and cook 10 kaffir lime leaves in the hot oil for 1 minute on low heat. Add the fish to the pan, cover with aluminum foil, and cook for 20 minutes in the oven. Remove the foil and sprinkle with the sel de Guérande. Serve in the ovenproof pan.

CHEF'S COMMENTS: I have replaced bay leaves with kaffir lime leaves in other recipes. The result is astonishing.

The skin and leaves of oriental limes are strong and have an intriguing flavor. You could use lemon or orange leaves.—**TRANS.**

Sole paprika

Filets de sole poêlés au paprika

SERVES 4

PREPARATION: 15 minutes
COOKING: 30 minutes

- 1½ pounds (600 g) sole fillets
- 1 red bell pepper
- 1 clove garlic
- Juice of ½ lemon
- 6 tablespoons (10 cl) fish stock (optional)
- 1 tablespoon paprika
- 3 tablespoons (6 cl) olive oil
- 7 tablespoons (3½ oz, 70 g) butter
- Salt, freshly ground pepper

Cut the red pepper in half and remove and seeds and interior veins. Cut into small pieces.

Heat a pan with half the olive oil and add the red pepper and unpeeled garlic. Season with salt. Cook for about 25 minutes, covered, over very low heat. Add 6 tablespoons of water halfway through the cooking.

Remove and discard the garlic. Add the red pepper to a blender along with the lemon juice, 3 tablespoons of very hot water, and the butter cut in small pieces. Blend for 30 seconds. Season with salt and pepper. If the sauce is too thick, thin it with water or fish stock.

In a nonstick pan, heat the rest of the olive oil. Sprinkle the paprika on the sole fillets, add salt and pepper. Cook the fillets for 5 minutes over high heat, turning halfway through.

Cover the fillets with the sauce and serve immediately. →

CHEF'S COMMENTS: Red bell pepper goes very well with fish. This blending of flavors is accentuated by the paprika, which is more often used with meat. Use the paprika moderately to give character to the fish.

Pureed bell pepper goes well with chicken and turkey. We like to use additional red pepper, as it serves as sauce and vegetable.—**TRANS.**

Whiting in an envelope with ginger and lemongrass
Merlan en papillote au gingembre et à la citronnelle

SERVES 4

PREPARATION: 15 minutes
COOKING: 25 minutes

- 4 whiting, about 1 pound each, cleaned
- 2 tomatoes, seeds removed, diced
- Juice of 1 lemon
- 2 ounces (50 g) fresh ginger, about a 3-inch piece
- 8 kaffir lime leaves (or, if not available, zest of 1 lime)
- 2 lemongrass bulbs
- 6 tablespoons (10 cl) olive oil
- Fine salt and fleur de sel

Preheat the oven to 350°F (180°C).

Make small incisions on each side of the whiting. Finely chop the lemongrass bulbs. Peel and grate the ginger. Set aside.

Cut aluminum foil into 4 rectangles 12 inches by 15 inches (30 by 40 cm). Put the tomatoes, ginger, lemongrass, and 1 kaffir lime leaf on half of each piece of foil. Season with salt. Add the fish and sprinkle with olive oil. Salt again and put 1 kaffir lime leaf on each fish. Sprinkle with lemon juice and seal the foil cases hermetically. Cook for 25 minutes in the oven and serve accompanied by the fleur de sel.

→

CHEF'S COMMENTS: All the flavors enclosed in the foil case penetrate the fish. The Chinese have similar recipes for fish and shellfish, steamed. The bulb of the lemongrass is all that is used for this recipe. You can use the stalk in an infusion.

Monkfish, cod, and other white fish will also do. If you do not make steamed fish oriental-style, you should.—**TRANS.**

Spiced crusted bream
Daurade panée aux épices concassées

SERVES 2

PREPARATION: 10 minutes
COOKING: 15 minutes

- 1 whole bream of about 2 pounds (800 g), cleaned and scaled
- ½ teaspoon coriander seed
- ½ teaspoon mustard seed
- ½ teaspoon caraway seed
- Juice of 1 lime
- 1 shallot, peeled and finely chopped
- 2 tablespoons (¾ oz, 20 g) tapenade of black olives
- 9 tablespoons (15 cl) olive oil
- ½ teaspoon fleur de sel

Put all the spices together on a cutting board or other hard surface and crush them gently with the bottom of a small pan. Sprinkle the bream with fleur de sel on both sides. Place the fish on the spices and press hard to make a crust of spices on the skin of the fish.

In a pan, combine the tapenade, lime juice, shallot, and 6 tablespoons (10 cl) of olive oil. Mix well and warm these ingredients for 10 seconds over low heat.

Heat the rest of the olive oil in a frying pan. When it is hot but not smoking, add the fish. Cook over low heat for 7 minutes on each side. Do not burn the spices, as this would give the dish a bitter taste.

When the bream is cooked, remove the fillets with the skin attached. Serve with a little tapenade sauce.

→

CHEF'S COMMENTS: While cooking this dish, there will be delicious odors. You can use other mixtures of spices, but don't use more than three or four varieties.

You can buy prepared tapenade; to make it yourself, crush pitted olives with some oil. A mortar and pestle can be used to crush the spices.—**TRANS.**

Swordfish crusted with poppy seeds

Tranche d'espadon en croûte de pavot

SERVES 4 | PREPARATION: 15 minutes
COOKING: 10 minutes

4 swordfish steaks
1 bulb fennel, trimmed and finely chopped
Juice of ½ lime
5 tablespoons (1 oz, 25 g) poppy seeds
6 tablespoons (10 cl) hazelnut oil
1 tablespoon olive oil
Salt

Boil the fennel in salted water for 5 minutes, then drain.

Heat the hazelnut oil, fennel, and lime juice in a small pan. Season with salt. Let warm slowly until the fish is cooked.

Spread the poppy seeds on a large plate. Salt the swordfish and cover evenly with the poppy seeds. Heat the olive oil in a nonstick pan large enough to hold all four steaks at once. Cook the fish for 2 minutes on each side.

Put the sauce on the plates, then add the fish. Serve immediately.

CHEF'S COMMENTS: The toasted poppy seeds will smell like hazelnuts and will crunch in your mouth. A real treat!

Remove the stalks and hard outside parts of the fennel and stew them with an onion as the basis for a broth or sauce.—**TRANS.**

Spicy fish stew

Pot-au-feu de poissons à la croque aux épices

SERVES 4	PREPARATION: 25 minutes COOKING: 25 minutes

Fillets of 2 red mullet (about 1 pound, 450 g)

2 slices of salmon (about 1 pound, 450 g)

2 carrots, peeled and cut in half lengthwise

2 bulbs fennel

2 leeks

1 pinch of thyme (preferably fresh)

1 bay leaf

4 cloves

½ tablespoon cumin seed

½ tablespoon coriander seed

½ tablespoon Szechuan pepper

2 tablespoons sea salt (fleur de sel)

1 tablespoon coarse salt

Trim the leeks, removing most of the green, and cut in half lengthwise. Wash carefully. Cut the fennel bulbs in two pieces.

Boil 3 quarts (3 liters) of water with the coarse salt, thyme, bay leaf, and cloves. Add the vegetables and cook 15 minutes over low heat. Drain the broth and set the vegetables aside, keeping them warm.

Cut the slices of salmon in half. Add the salmon and red mullet to the vegetable broth. Simmer for 8 minutes, without boiling.

Put the vegetables in soup plates and add the fish. Mix the spices with the fleur de sel and sprinkle over the stew. Serve at the table with the remaining spices.

CHEF'S COMMENTS: The spice seeds, as you bite into them, add a fascinating variety of flavors to the stew.

Red snapper could replace the mullet. Basically, you need a flavor that contrasts with the salmon, preferably a fish that does not flake when cooked. Szechuan is a Chinese pepper, not difficult to find.

We like the combination of spices in this recipe so much that we use it regularly on the table instead of just salt and pepper as a seasoning for many dishes. The large fillets used in the recipe look good in a large, flat soup dish, but smaller pieces are more practical.—**TRANS.**

Glazed mackerel with black pepper
Maquereaux laqués au poivre noir

SERVES 4

PREPARATION: 15 minutes
COOKING: 10 minutes

4 mackerel fillets of about 6 ounces (150 g) each
1 tablespoon white vinegar
1 tablespoon soy sauce
2 tablespoons sugar
1 tablespoon black peppercorns

Remove all the small bones from the fillets with a tweezer.

Have 6 tablespoons (10 cl) of cold water ready. Heat the sugar in a nonstick pan to caramelize it. Deglaze with the water, vinegar, and soy sauce. Dilute the caramel for 1 minute, still boiling. Add the mackerel to the pan, skin side down. Cook for 2 minutes over low heat, then turn and cook for 1 more minute.

Change the grind of your pepper mill to grind the pepper a bit larger than the size of a sesame seed. Grind several turns of pepper over each fillet and serve.

CHEF'S COMMENTS: The Japanese use this glazing technique for many grilled fish dishes and also for meat.

This is an excellent recipe. Sardines, red mullet, and snapper can also be used. Although most supermarkets carry coarsely ground pepper, freshly ground is better.—**TRANS.**

Cabbage stuffed with skate, tomato, and coriander

Raie en chou farci, tomate à la coriandre

SERVES 4

PREPARATION: 45 minutes
COOKING: 35 minutes

- 1½ pounds (700 g) skate, whole
- 1 green cabbage
- 4 tomatoes, seeded and cut into large pieces
- Juice of ½ lemon
- 1 shallot
- 1 onion, peeled
- 1 sprig thyme
- 1 bay leaf
- 2 cloves
- 10 coriander seeds
- ½ teaspoon powdered coriander
- 3 tablespoons (5 cl) olive oil
- 4 tablespoons (2 oz, 50 g) butter
- Coarse salt, fine salt

Preheat the oven to 250°F (120°C).

Puree the tomatoes in a blender with the olive oil, then pour the puree through a sieve. In a pan, combine the tomato puree, coriander seeds, and salt. Cook for 5 minutes over low heat, then whisk in half the butter. Set aside.

Put the skate, onion, thyme, bay leaf, cloves, and lemon juice in a large pan with a pinch of coarse salt. Cover with water. Cook for 20 minutes over low heat. Take out the skate, remove the skin, and break the flesh into pieces. →

Wash and separate the cabbage leaves. Put 4 large leaves in a large pan with salted water and boil for 1 minute, then plunge them into cold water and drain. Cut the rest of the cabbage in ½-inch (1 cm) strips. Blanch for 1 minute, then put into cold water. Press the strips with your hands to extract the water.

Melt the rest of the butter in a pan and toss the cabbage strips in it. Sprinkle with powdered coriander and salt. After 2 minutes add the skate. Mix and cook for 2 minutes. Spread out the cooked cabbage leaves and divide the skate mixture onto each. Close the leaves to form small packages and cook for 5 minutes in the oven. Put each leaf on a plate, coat with the tomato puree, and garnish with a pinch of powdered coriander.

CHEF'S COMMENTS: The tomato adds a touch of acidity which skate needs. The appetite is stimulated by the odor of the powdered coriander at the last minute.

You could try this with shark.—**TRANS.**

Scallop of monkfish with eggplant and spiced sweet potatoes

Paupiettes de lotte à l'aubergine, patate douce aux épices

SERVES 4	PREPARATION: 25 minutes COOKING: 20 minutes

1¼ pounds (600 g) monkfish, trimmed and cleaned and cut into 8 slices
2 large eggplants
1 sweet potato, peeled and cut into small dice
2 tablespoons chopped almonds
½ teaspoon black sesame seeds
½ teaspoon sumac (or paprika)
½ teaspoon cumin seeds
¾ cup (20 cl) olive oil
2 tablespoons fleur de sel
1 tablespoon balsamic vinegar
Fine salt, freshly ground pepper

Preheat the oven to 250°F (120°C).

Wash the eggplants and cut them lengthwise into 8 slices of about ¼ inch (5 mm). Salt the slices on both sides. Heat olive oil in a pan and cook each slice 5 minutes on each side. Drain on paper towels.

Season the monkfish with salt and pepper and in a pan heated with olive oil brown 2 minutes on each side. Set aside.

Sauté the sweet potato in a little olive oil for 1 minute. Add the almonds, cumin, and sesame seeds. Cook 1 more minute. Set aside. →

Wrap each piece of monkfish in a slice of eggplant and put in an ovenproof dish. Cover with the sweet potato mixture and bake for 5 minutes.

Mix the olive oil with the balsamic vinegar. Add salt and pepper. When the fish is taken out of the oven, add the vinaigrette, sprinkle with sumac and fleur de sel, and serve immediately.

CHEF'S COMMENTS: Be careful to measure the spices well so that the cumin, which is stronger, doesn't overwhelm the others.

Salting eggplant in advance removes some water and makes the flesh softer. It will absorb less oil or fat.—**TRANS.**

Pollack with potatoes and star anise
Lieu jaune au lait de pomme de terre et à l'anis étoilé

SERVES 4 | PREPARATION: 15 minutes
COOKING: 25 minutes

4 pollack steaks, 5 ounces each
½ pound (250 g) larger potatoes, a bit floury
5 star anise
5 ounces (15 cl) whipping (heavy) cream
3 cups (75 cl) milk
2 tablespoons olive oil
4 tablespoons (2 oz, 50 g) butter
Salt

Peel and wash the potatoes and cut each into two pieces. Put in a pan with the milk, cream and star anise. Cook for 15 minutes over low heat, then put in a blender with the butter. Puree until smooth. Pour through a fine sieve into a pan and keep hot. Salt to taste. If the sauce is too thick, add a little milk.

Heat the olive oil in a nonstick pan. Add the pollack and brown for 5 minutes on each side.

Put the potato puree into four shallow dishes and add the fish. Serve hot.

CHEF'S COMMENTS: The anise adds flavor to the neutral taste of the potatoes. Choose thick fish steaks so that they keep tender.

Basically a thick white fish fillet on a flavored potato puree. The thickness of the fish is more important than its kind.—**TRANS.**

Steamed shrimp with ginger
Gambas à la vapeur de gingembre

SERVES 4	PREPARATION: 40 minutes COOKING: 10 minutes

- 2¼ pounds (1 kg) large shrimp (about 3 oz each)
- 2 cloves garlic, chopped
- 1 bunch cilantro, chopped
- 2 ounces (50 g) fresh ginger, about a 3-inch piece, finely grated
- 3 ounces (10 cl) soy sauce
- 1 tablespoon toasted sesame oil
- 3 tablespoons peanut oil

Cut the shrimp lengthwise into 2 pieces. With the point of a knife, remove the black vein and the pouch in the head, then put the shrimp into two shallow bowls.

Boil water in a steamer. Heat the two oils in a pan and add the ginger and the garlic. Cook over low heat for 15 seconds. Add the soy sauce and 3 ounces (10 cl) of water and bring to a boil.

Pour this sauce on the shrimp and put one soup bowl in the steamer. Cook covered for 10 minutes. Then steam the other bowl. Sprinkle with cilantro and serve.

CHEF'S COMMENTS: This dish comes directly from the culinary repertory of Southeast Asia, where steaming is the best way to cook seafood. Young ginger can be found in Asian supermarkets. It is cream colored with pink tips; don't confuse it with fresh galanga which it resembles. As it is delicate and crunchy, you can use more of it than ripe ginger.

If you can't find young ginger, fresh ripe ginger or galanga can be used.—**TRANS.**

Cod and red lentil stew
Cabillaud et lentilles roses compotés aux épices

SERVES 4	PREPARATION: 15 minutes COOKING: 30 minutes

2 pounds (800 g) cod fillets, skin removed, cut into 1-inch (2 cm) pieces (or substitute pollack or whiting)
18 ounces (500 g) red lentils
1 onion, chopped
1 clove garlic, finely sliced
1 sprig thyme
1 bay leaf
3 star anise
½ teaspoon powdered cumin (or garam masala)
3 tablespoons (5 cl) olive oil
Salt, finely ground pepper

Heat olive oil in a pan and brown the onion, garlic, and star anise for 1 minute over low heat. Add the lentils. Stir for 30 seconds with a wooden spoon, then add the powdered cumin.

Add the fish to the lentils and cover with 1 quart (1 liter) of water. Add the thyme and bay leaf and cook covered over low heat for 20 minutes. When the lentils are cooked, remove the thyme and bay leaf and mix well. The water should be completely absorbed and the lentils well cooked. Season with salt and pepper, mix for 1 minute, cover, and let it stand for 10 minutes off the heat. Serve warm with a good olive oil.

You can accompany this dish with a salad dressed with olive oil and lemon juice. →

CHEF'S COMMENTS: This rustic dish is easy to make, and the flavor of spices will take your imagination to exotic places. Star anise, after cooking, has a delicate flavor: its heavy flavor when not cooked will have totally disappeared.

Red lentils tend to be Turkish rather than French. Lentils have been popular lately in Paris with such meats as haddock and foie gras. Just follow the above recipe without the star anise and cumin.—**TRANS.**

Gray mullet roasted with orange and cinnamon
Mulet rôti au four à l'orange et à la cannelle

SERVES 6

PREPARATION: 10 minutes
COOKING: 20 minutes

A mullet of 3 pounds (1.5 kg), scaled and cleaned
1 untreated orange
5 cloves garlic, unpeeled
Juice of ½ lemon
4 sticks of cinnamon
½ teaspoon powdered cinnamon
6 tablespoons (10 cl) olive oil
2 tablespoons (1 oz, 20 g) butter

Preheat the oven to 350°F (180°C).

Wash and dry the orange. Cut it in slices without peeling and put the slices in an ovenproof pan.

With a sharp knife make deep slashes on each side of the fish, and insert the cinnamon sticks. Put the fish on the orange slices and moisten with olive oil. Pour 10 ounces (30 cl) of water over the fish and place the garlic next to the fish. Bake for 20 minutes.

Remove the fish from the pan. Add the butter and powdered cinnamon to the pan and mix well. Add the lemon juice. Put the fish back in the pan and serve immediately.

CHEF'S COMMENTS: Mullet is an often forgotten fish, but it has many good qualities. You must check that it doesn't get dry. →

Here you will discover cinnamon in a savory rather than a sweet dish. Surprisingly, its flavor goes well with fish. You can try this with cod, pollack, or other white fish.

One of the standbys at Le Pré Verre is cod roasted with cinnamon sticks, served with a smoked potato puree.—**TRANS.**

Casserole of monkfish with Chinese cinnamon
Queue de lotte en cocotte à la cannelle de Chine

SERVES 6

PREPARATION: 20 minutes
COOKING: 25 minutes

1 monkfish tail, about 3 pounds (1.5 kg), skin removed
2 lemons
2 cloves garlic, peeled
1 piece of fresh ginger the size of a walnut, peeled and cut in strips
5 sticks of cassia (Chinese cinnamon), or cinnamon
½ teaspoon powdered cinnamon
6 tablespoons (10 cl) olive oil
Sel de Guérande

Preheat the oven to 350°F (180°C).

Remove the lemon zests with a peeler and put them in a pan. Cover with a quart of water and cook for 5 minutes. Juice one of the lemons and set aside.

Heat the olive oil in a cast-iron casserole. Add the cinnamon sticks and cook, stirring, for 15 seconds. Add the monkfish and brown on all sides. Add the garlic, ginger, lemon zests, and powdered cinnamon. Cover and cook in the oven for 20 minutes, basting regularly.

Remove from oven and moisten the fish with the lemon juice. Let stand for 5 minutes so that the cooking juices come →

slowly to the surface. Serve in the casserole, sprinkled with sel de Guérande.

CHEF'S COMMENTS: The cassia, much used in China, is excellent when cooking fish. Its flavor melts into the dish.

When using smaller tails of monkfish, reduce the cooking time.—**TRANS.**

Scorpion fish with fennel and sumac

Filets de rascasse au fenouil et au sumac

SERVES 4	PREPARATION: 25 minutes COOKING: 30 minutes

4 scorpion fish fillets
10 black olives, pitted
Juice of ½ lemon
1 bulb fennel, cut into strips
1 small onion, chopped
1 small clove garlic, peeled and thinly sliced
1 tablespoon sumac (if not available, substitute paprika)
½ teaspoon fennel seed
¾ cup (20 cl) olive oil
Salt

Heat 6 tablespoons (10 cl) of olive oil in a large pot and add the onion and garlic. Cook over low heat for 1 minute. Add the fennel and moisten with ¾ cup (20 cl) water. Cook, covered, for 20 minutes, then blend to obtain a smooth puree.

Chop the olives, cover with cold water in a pan, and bring to a boil. Dry them and add to the fennel sauce. Add the lemon juice and the fennel seed. Cook for 2 minutes and add salt.

Heat the rest of the olive oil in a frying pan and cook the fish fillets for 3 minutes on each side. Pour the sauce on plates and add the fish on top. Serve immediately.

CHEF'S COMMENTS: Sumac has been used since antiquity and now has many uses in Turkey and Iran, especially for →

seasoning fish. Its slightly acidic and fruity taste brings out flavors in an original fashion.

A rascasse is a scorpion fish or ocean perch, but redfish or snapper could be used. Sumac, a biblical spice, also goes well with onions and chicken for various Middle Eastern dishes.—**TRANS.**

Sea bass in a spicy broth
Bar au court-bouillon d'épices

SERVES 4 | PREPARATION: 15 minutes
COOKING: 40 minutes

- 1 sea bass, about 3 pounds (1.5 kg), scaled and cleaned
- 1 carrot
- 1 leek
- 1 bulb fennel
- 1 onion
- ½ stalk celery
- 3 star anise
- 1 stick cinnamon
- 5 cloves
- ½ teaspoon dill seed
- ½ teaspoon coriander seeds
- ½ teaspoon fenugreek seeds
- 2 teaspoons gray coarse sea salt

Peel and wash the vegetables and cut them into small dice. Put them in a pan and cover with 3 quarts (3 liters) of water. Bring to a boil and cook for 20 minutes. Then add all the spices, salt, and let cook for 10 more minutes.

Put the whole sea bass into this court-bouillon, bring to a boil, and remove from the heat. Let the fish poach in the bouillon for 10 minutes. Remove the fish and serve right away, with a splash of olive oil.

→

CHEF'S COMMENTS: This light infusion of spices adds subtle flavors to the flesh of the sea bass. You can use this court-bouillon with other fish, poaching for 5 minutes for each pound (500 g) of weight. The fish keeps all its texture. A real treat!

We usually strain the court-bouillon and find another use for it, such as a soup.—**TRANS.**

6 Meats

Veal kidneys with ginger and juniper berries
Rognons de veau au gingembre et aux baies de genièvre

SERVES 2	PREPARATION: 25 minutes COOKING: 10 minutes

2 whole veal kidneys, with the fat removed
¼ pound (100 g) shallots, finely chopped
8 juniper berries
½ ounce (10 g) fresh ginger, about a ½-inch piece
1 tablespoon lemon juice
¼ teaspoon brown sugar
3 tablespoons (5 cl) peanut oil
Salt, freshly ground black pepper

Preheat the oven to 350°F (180°C).

Cut the ginger in thin slices, then in sticks, and then cut into small cubes. Set aside.

Sweat the shallots in a little oil. Add the ginger, sugar, and juniper berries. Cook for 10 seconds over low heat, while stirring. As soon as a light caramelization appears, add the lemon juice, bring to a boil, and season with salt and pepper.

Heat the rest of the oil in an ovenproof pan. Salt the kidneys. When the oil is hot, add the kidneys, open face side up, and brown for 3 minutes. Turn the kidneys and cook them in the oven for 5 minutes, until they become pinkish.

Remove from the oven and let them stand for 2 minutes on a crumpled piece of aluminum foil, so that they are not →

soaked by their juices. Put them on plates and cover with the shallot sauce. Serve immediately.

CHEF'S COMMENTS: This gentle cooking in the oven keeps the kidneys tender. The juniper berries add a complementary freshness to the taste of the peppery ginger.

Do not overcook kidneys or livers, as they toughen.—**TRANS.**

Scallop of veal with garam masala

Escalope de veau au garam masala

SERVES 4 | PREPARATION: 20 minutes
COOKING: 10 minutes

- 4 scallops of veal, each about 6 ounces (180 g)
- 1 stalk celery, peeled to remove fibers, diced
- Juice of ½ lemon
- ½ teaspoon garam masala (or cumin or powdered coriander)
- 3 tablespoons (5 cl) peanut oil
- 4 tablespoons (2 oz, 50 g) butter
- Pinch of sugar
- Salt, freshly ground pepper

Bring a small pan of salted water to a boil. Plunge the celery into the boiling water for 30 seconds, then drain.

Heat the oil in a nonstick pan and brown the scallops for 2 minutes on each side. Put them in a serving dish.

Discard the cooking oil and put the pan on a rather high heat. Add 3 ounces (10 cl) of cold water and scrape the pan to loosen the juices. Reduce by half. Add the garam masala, lemon juice, sugar, and butter, and stir until the butter is melted. Add a tablespoon of water to thin the sauce. Add the celery, salt, and pepper. Bring to boil for 5 seconds and pour over the veal. Serve right away.

CHEF'S COMMENTS: Garam masala is a mixture of sweet spices from northern India. When it is of good quality (that is, freshly ground) its flavors are subtle and add a marvelous touch to dishes. You can find it in good oriental shops, especially Indian shops.

For those semi-vegetarians who do not eat four-legged animals, turkey or chicken could be substituted for the veal.—**TRANS.**

Beef knuckle with coconut and lemongrass
Jarret de boeuf à la noix de coco et à la citronnelle

SERVES 4

PREPARATION: 20 minutes
COOKING: 1 hour 40 minutes

- 2¼ pounds (1 kg) of beef knuckle or cheek, cut into 1-inch (2 cm) cubes
- 4 cups (14 oz, 400 g) dried grated unsweetened coconut
- 2 onions, finely chopped
- 1 to 2 hot peppers (optional)
- 2 stalks lemongrass, each cut into 4 pieces
- ¾ ounce (20 g) fresh ginger, about a 1½-inch piece, grated
- 1 tablespoon brown sugar
- 6 tablespoons (10 cl) peanut oil
- Gros sel, fine salt
- Freshly ground black pepper

Soak the coconut in 2½ quarts (2.5 liters) of hot water. Process the coconut with the water in a blender (be careful not to overfill—blend in two lots if necessary). Put this mixture through a fine sieve, pressing to extract all the coconut milk. (You could boil the coconut and water for 2 minutes before blending to extract more milk.) Save 3 tablespoons of grated coconut from the sieve.

Heat the oil in a cast-iron pot and brown the meat. Add the ginger, onions, sugar, lemongrass, 3 tablespoons of grated coconut, and the hot peppers (if you use them). Cook slowly to brown, then add the coconut milk and a pinch of gros sel. Cook covered for 1 hour and uncovered for 30 minutes to thicken and reduce the sauce. Pierce the meat with the point of a knife to see if it is done.

If it is not yet very soft, add a glass of water and cook 10 more minutes. Add salt and pepper, and serve.

CHEF'S COMMENTS: To make this dish I have adapted a Malaysian recipe called *rendang*. If you use the hot pepper in this dish, it is better to serve it lukewarm.

One learns from this about using grated coconut as a thickening for stews.—**TRANS.**

Veal in a white sauce with star anise and spices
Blanquette de veau aux épices anisées

SERVES 4	PREPARATION: 20 minutes COOKING: 60 minutes

2¼ pounds (1 kg) veal shoulder, bones removed, cut into 1-inch (2 cm) cubes
2 carrots, peeled and cut into rounds
1 onion, peeled and quartered
1 leek, split, washed carefully, and finely chopped
2 cloves
3 star anise
5 white or green cardamom seeds
2 tablespoons (1 oz, 30 g) flour
3 tablespoons (5 cl) crème fraîche
4 tablespoons (2 oz, 50 g) butter
Coarse salt and fine salt

Cover the meat with 2 quarts (2 liters) of cold water, add the onion, carrots, leek, cloves, star anise, and a pinch of coarse salt. Bring to a boil, lower the heat, and cook 45 minutes over low heat. This liquid will give you a bouillon to make the sauce.

To make the white sauce, cook the butter with the cardamom in a medium-sized pan for a minute over low heat. Whisk in the flour, add approximately 1 cup (25 cl) of the veal bouillon, and whisk again when it boils. Add another cup of the bouillon, whisk, and boil. Add the crème fraîche and the clove and star anise from the leftover bouillon, and cook 5 minutes over low heat. (You can cook rice or vegetables in the remaining bouillon to accompany the veal.)

Add the veal to the sauce and heat for 5 minutes. Correct the seasoning and serve hot.

CHEF'S COMMENTS: You will appreciate this version of blanquette, with its peppery and anise flavors, any time of the year.

This recipe could also be used with chicken or turkey, cooked for less time.—**TRANS.**

Spiced leg of lamb
Gigot d'agneau confit aux épices

SERVES 5 to 6	PREPARATION: 15 minutes MARINATING: 30 minutes COOKING: 2 hours

1 leg of lamb about 4½ pounds (2 kg)
4 onions, chopped
1 tablespoon dill seed (or fennel seed)
3 tablespoons powdered coriander
1 tablespoon powdered cumin
2 sticks cinnamon
5 tablespoons soy sauce
3 tablespoons (5 cl) peanut oil
4 tablespoons (2 oz, 50 g) butter
2 tablespoons sugar
1 tablespoon freshly ground pepper
Salt

This dish is made with a pressure cooker. If your pressure cooker is too small, trim the lamb to shorten it.

Cut small slashes in the leg of lamb with a knife. Mix the dill seed, coriander, cumin, soy sauce, ground pepper, and sugar, and rub the leg of lamb with this mixture. Let it marinate for 30 minutes in the refrigerator.

In the pressure cooker, heat the oil and brown the lamb on all sides. Add the onion, cook lightly, then add water and the cinnamon sticks. If your leg of lamb is between 3 and 4½ pounds (1.5 and 2 kg) add 1½ quarts (1.5 liters) water. Cook for an hour and a half to an hour and three quarters. At this point check the water level, since evaporation varies according to cooking temperature. Continue cooking covered, having added perhaps a bit of water.

When the leg of lamb is cooked, turn off the heat and release the pressure. When all the steam is gone, remove the lamb and put it on a serving dish. Reduce the juice on the heat to get 8 ounces (25 cl) of liquid. Whisk in the butter, then add salt and pepper. Serve with the sauce on the side.

CHEF'S COMMENTS: This is a well-cooked leg of lamb that can be eaten with a spoon. The spices mixed with soy sauce produce a caramelized taste that goes perfectly with the lamb.

This is an interesting, speeded-up version of the seven-hour leg of lamb popular in France.—**TRANS.**

Sautéed rabbit with cumin

Sauté de lapin au cumin

SERVES 4 to 6	PREPARATION: 30 minutes COOKING: 50 minutes

- 1 rabbit of 4½ pounds (2 kg), cut into pieces
- 5 cloves garlic, unpeeled
- 2 onions, chopped
- 1 sprig of thyme
- 1 bay leaf
- Juice of ½ lemon
- 2 tablespoons powdered cumin
- ½ teaspoon cumin seed
- 2 cups (50 cl) dry white wine
- 2 tablespoons crème fraîche
- 2 tablespoons flour
- 3 tablespoons (5 cl) peanut oil
- Salt, freshly ground gray pepper

Salt and pepper the pieces of rabbit. Heat a little oil in a pan and brown the rabbit gently, taking care not to dry out the flesh. When the pieces are nicely colored, drain in a sieve.

In a casserole with a heavy bottom, heat a little oil, add the onions, thyme, bay leaf, and garlic. Cook for 5 minutes without browning. Add the rabbit and mix well. Sprinkle with cumin (powder and seeds) and cook, stirring, for 2 minutes over low heat. Sprinkle with flour, stirring, then add the white wine and 2 cups (50 cl) of water. There should be enough liquid to cover the rabbit. Cook covered for 45 minutes over low heat.

When the rabbit is cooked, add the lemon juice and check the seasoning. Mix in the crème fraîche and bring to a boil. Take to the table in the casserole.

CHEF'S COMMENTS: This is the classic sautéed rabbit that our grandmothers used to make, brought up to date with a touch of cumin. You will discover rabbit anew!

The tender-hearted might try this with chicken legs.—**TRANS.**

Roast pork with cumin
Rôti de porc au cumin

SERVES 4	PREPARATION: 15 minutes COOKING: 1 hour 45 minutes

1 pork roast, 2 pounds (800 to 900 g), prepared by the butcher
2 onions, chopped
4 cloves garlic, unpeeled
1 sprig thyme
1 bay leaf
5 cloves
10 black peppercorns
2 tablespoons cumin seeds
2 tablespoons powdered cumin
6 tablespoons (10 cl) white wine
¾ cup (20 cl) crème fraîche
1 tablespoon (½ oz, 10 g) butter
3 tablespoons (5 cl) peanut oil
Coarse salt, fine salt
Freshly ground pepper

Preheat the oven to 400°F (200°C).

Put the pork in a large pan and cover it with cold water, thyme, bay leaf, cloves, peppercorns, and a pinch of coarse salt. Bring to a boil and simmer for 50 minutes. Remove the pork and drain on a rack for 30 minutes, then cover with cumin seed.

Put the peanut oil on a flat, ovenproof pan and heat in the oven.

Sprinkle the pork with half the cumin powder and a little fine salt. Brown on all sides in the flat pan, then roast in the oven for 20 minutes with the whole unpeeled garlic cloves.

Heat the butter in a frying pan. Add the onions and sweat for 5 minutes over low heat. Add the rest of the cumin powder and the white wine and cook to reduce to about 1 tablespoon. Add the crème fraîche and simmer for 2 minutes. Add salt and pepper.

Remove the roast from the oven and slice it. Cover with the cumin sauce just before serving.

CHEF'S COMMENTS: The oriental accent of cumin will make a simple roast pork into a flavorful and original dish.

You could substitute yogurt for the crème fraîche, being careful not to cover the pan, as the sauce will curdle.—**TRANS.**

Shoulder of lamb with star anise
Épaule d'agneau fondante à l'anis étoilé

SERVES 6

PREPARATION: 30 minutes
COOKING: 1 hour 30 minutes
REFRIGERATION: 12 hours

1 lamb shoulder of about 2½ pounds (1.2 kg), deboned and rolled
1 onion
1 carrot
1 bulb fennel
10 star anise
2 cups (50 cl) dry white wine
1 tablespoon brown sugar
2 tablespoons flour
2 tablespoons crème fraîche
3 tablespoons peanut oil
Fine salt

Peel and wash the vegetables. Cut them into ½-inch dice. In a cast-iron casserole, brown them gently with half the peanut oil. Add 5 star anise.

In a frying pan, brown the lamb shoulder on all sides. Transfer the meat to the casserole and sprinkle with flour. Moisten with the white wine and 2 cups (50 cl) of water. Add the sugar and a pinch of salt. Bring to a boil, cover, and cook on medium heat for 30 minutes. Turn the lamb over and cook for another 30 minutes. Add the remaining 5 star anise and, if needed, water to cover the meat. Cook another 30 minutes. When the meat is done, a fork should go in easily.

When the pork has cooled a bit, roll it tightly in plastic wrap and refrigerate for 12 hours. Put the cooking juices through a sieve and save, refrigerated. Remove the star anise.

The next day, remove the plastic wrap and cut the meat in 1-inch (2 cm) slices. Heat these in a little oil. Heat the sauce gently and serve on the side.

CHEF'S COMMENTS: Chinese cuisine uses a lot of star anise, especially with pork dishes. Lamb also goes well with the anise flavors.

A useful dish to make a day in advance, especially when guests are coming.—**TRANS.**

Rabbit legs with green aniseed
Cuisses de lapin à l'anis vert

SERVES 4	PREPARATION: 30 minutes COOKING: 45 minutes

- 4 rabbit legs
- 2 limes
- 1 onion, thinly sliced
- 2 cloves garlic, unpeeled
- 4 tablespoons green aniseed (or fennel seed)
- 4 tablespoons (1 oz, 20 g) flour
- 1 tablespoon (½ oz, 10 g) butter
- ½ teaspoon sugar
- 2 tablespoons peanut oil
- Fine salt

Peel the limes with a vegetable peeler and boil the peels in water for 5 minutes. Squeeze one of the limes. In a heavy-bottom pan, heat the oil and butter. Salt the rabbit legs and brown slowly on all sides. Then add the onion, the unpeeled garlic, the aniseed, sugar, and lime peel. Cook for about 1 minute. Sprinkle with flour and moisten with 2 cups (50 cl) of water. Add salt and the juice of 1 lime. Bring to a boil, cover, and cook for an hour over low heat.

Check the seasoning and serve immediately.

CHEF'S COMMENTS: Green aniseed has a less strong flavor than star anise. The little seeds crunch between your teeth when eaten, adding to the flavor of the dish.

Many of the dishes use spices for texture as well as flavor.—**TRANS.**

Spiced pork belly

Poitrine de porc fondante aux trois épices

SERVES 4 to 5	PREPARATION: 30 minutes COOKING: 1 hour 20 minutes

- 2¼ pounds (1 kg) fresh lean pork belly, cut into 1-inch (2 cm) slices (ask your butcher to do this)
- 1 large onion
- 1 carrot
- 1 stalk celery
- 2 stalks of Ceylanese cinnamon
- 8 pieces of star anise
- 8 pieces of long pepper (or substitute one whole vanilla bean)
- 1½ cups (40 cl) crème fraîche
- Fine salt

Peel and wash the vegetables and chop coarsely. Put into a pot with the meat and spices. Cover with water and bring to a boil. Lower the heat and cook for about 1 hour, covered. Prick the meat with a fork to be sure it's tender. Remove the meat. Sieve the broth, take out the vegetables, then reduce to about ¾ cup (20 cl). Add the crème fraîche and cook for 5 minutes. Then add the meat and spices and cook slowly until the cream thickens. Add salt and serve very hot.

CHEF'S COMMENTS: Ceylanese cinnamon (in long, light, crumbly sticks) is best here. Its delicate flavor goes well with the melted spices in this dish. I like to serve it with crunchy green cabbage. Long pepper adds a spicy vanilla note to the dish. Take care to leave the pepper whole.

Fillet of pork with caramelized star anise
Filet mignon de porc au caramel d'anis étoilé

SERVES 4 | PREPARATION: 30 minutes
COOKING: 20 minutes

- 2 pork fillets
- 6 star anise
- 1 tablespoon vinegar
- 2 tablespoons (1 oz, 25 g) butter
- 1½ tablespoons (¾ oz, 20 g) sugar
- 1 tablespoon cornstarch
- 3 tablespoons (5 cl) peanut oil
- Fine salt, freshly ground white pepper

Heat the oil in a frying pan. Salt and pepper the pork fillets and brown gently. Cover and cook for 10 minutes, turning after 5 minutes.

In a saucepan, bring the star anise to boil with 2 cups of water, and reduce to ¾ cup (20 cl).

Heat the sugar in a small pan and stir with a wooden spoon to make a caramel. Pour the infusion of star anise and the vinegar over the caramel and cook, stirring, for 5 minutes to dissolve the sugar.

Mix the cornstarch with 3 tablespoons cold water.

Remove the pork fillets and cut them in slices. Put onto 4 plates or a serving dish. Throw out the cooking oil. Put the caramel through a sieve, then put in a pan and bring to a boil. Whisk in the cornstarch and then incorporate the butter, cut in pieces. Add salt and pepper. Decorate the dish with the star anise and coat with the sauce.

CHEF'S COMMENTS: The Chinese adore star anise with pork. This is my interpretation of their influence.

This recipe could also be used with turkey fillets cut from the breast.—**TRANS.**

Shoulder of beef braised in white Anjou wine and mixed peppers
Paleron braisé au vin blanc d'Anjou et aux épices poivrées

SERVES 6	PREPARATION: 25 minutes COOKING: 1 hour 30 minutes

2 pounds (800 g) beef shoulder, in one piece, with fat removed
3 carrots, cut into thick slices
1 onion, chopped
2 cloves garlic, quartered
2 ounces (50 g) fresh ginger, about a 3-inch piece, sliced
2 cloves long pepper, crushed (or 1 nutmeg, grated)
1 tablespoon white peppercorns, crushed
2 cups (50 cl) Coteaux du Layon
2 cups (50 cl) white Anjou wine
3 tablespoons (5 cl) peanut oil
Salt

Heat the oil in a cast-iron pot. Brown the meat on all sides. Add the vegetables, then the white pepper and long pepper. Cook, stirring, for 5 minutes. Add the two wines and 2 cups (50 cl) of water. Salt lightly. Cover the pot, lower the heat, and stew for 90 minutes. If the meat is not tender by then, add a cup of water and continue cooking for 15 minutes.

At the end of the cooking time, remove the meat and reduce the cooking liquid to about ¾ cup (20 cl). If you want the dish rustic, keep the spices in the juice; if not, filter them out. Serve warm.

CHEF'S COMMENTS: Long pepper is a miracle spice that has a wide range of flavors. If you have difficulty finding it, replace it with black pepper, a little grated nutmeg, and half a vanilla bean at the end of the cooking.

Coteaux du Layon is a sweet white wine from Anjou. Substitute a sweet Chenin. For the white Anjou substitute a dry white Chardonnay or Sauvignon. For the reduction to ¾ cup, boil hard.—**TRANS.**

Ground veal with lemongrass
Tartare de veau à la citronnelle

SERVES 4 | PREPARATION: 20 minutes
REFRIGERATION: 1 hour

1¼ pounds (600 g) ground lean veal
1 shallot, chopped
5 tablespoons curly parsley, chopped
Juice of ½ lemon
2 stalks lemongrass
2 egg yolks
1 tablespoon thick crème fraîche
1 tablespoon strong mustard à l'ancienne
2 tablespoons olive oil
Salt, freshly ground pepper

Cut the lemongrass in fine slices (only the bulb; the rest of the stalk can be used for an infusion or in a court-bouillon). In a blender, puree the shallot and lemongrass.

Mix the egg yolks, mustard, and olive oil in a bowl. Add the lemon juice, parsley, and the lemongrass and shallot mixture. Mix well, adding the meat then the crème fraîche. Add salt and pepper. Refrigerate for 1 hour before serving.

This dish can be accompanied by a good salad of rocket (arugula), lamb's lettuce or red endive (trévise).

CHEF'S COMMENTS: The herbs and spices stand out here, as the veal does not have a strong taste. The flavor of the lemongrass dominates.

As with steak tartar, the veal is eaten raw. While the lemon juice and mustard cook the meat somewhat, you can also make patties and brown them slightly on both sides. Make certain the meat is freshly ground and not frozen.—**TRANS.**

Veal goulash with pistachios
Goulasch de veau aux pistaches

SERVES 4

PREPARATION: 40 minutes
COOKING: 1 hour 15 minutes

- 28 ounces (800 g) of veal (flank, shoulder, collar), cut into 1-inch (2 cm) cubes
- 4 tomatoes, cut into large dice
- 1 onion, chopped
- 1 clove garlic, sliced
- 1 cup (3½ oz, 100 g) shelled pistachios
- 1 bunch chives
- 2 tablespoons paprika
- 1 tablespoon tomato paste
- 6 tablespoons (10 cl) dry white wine
- 2 tablespoons wine vinegar
- 1 tablespoon crème fraîche
- 3 tablespoons (5 cl) peanut oil
- ½ teaspoon sugar
- Salt

Preheat the oven to 350°F (180°C).

In a ovenproof cast-iron pot heat the oil and brown the veal. Add the onion and garlic and cook 1 minute. Add the sugar and vinegar and cook another minute. Add the white wine, tomatoes, tomato paste, paprika, and salt. Moisten with 2 cups water and cook for 1 hour in the oven, covered.

Remove from the oven and cook over low heat for 15 minutes. Check the seasoning, then add the crème fraîche and pistachios. Cut the chives and sprinkle on the goulash just before serving.

CHEF'S COMMENTS: Buy the best paprika, preferably from Hungary, the most freshly milled possible (judge by the color and odor), and in a metal container. You could add potatoes to the stew halfway through the cooking, adding a glass of water.

If substituting chicken, turkey, or duck, you will need less cooking time.—**TRANS.**

7 Poultry

Duckling in honey and African pepper
Canette fermière au miel et à la maniguette

SERVES 4 | PREPARATION: 30 minutes
COOKING: 30 minutes

- 1 free-range duck
- 6 tablespoons (10 cl) sherry vinegar
- 3½ tablespoons (1½ oz, 50 g) acacia honey (or pine honey)
- 1 tablespoon Maniguette pepper (or, if not available, Szechuan pepper)
- 1 tablespoon sesame seeds
- ½ teaspoon cornstarch
- 4 tablespoons (2 oz, 50 g) butter
- tablespoons (5 cl) peanut oil
- Salt

Preheat the oven to 400°F (200°C).

In a saucepan, heat the honey until it caramelizes lightly. Then add the vinegar and cook for 1 minute over low heat.

Lightly toast the sesame seeds in a dry pan, stirring constantly. Add to the honey mixture.

In a pepper mill or blender, grind the Maniguette as finely as possible.

Heat the olive oil over medium heat in an ovenproof pan. Salt the duck and rub in some Maniguette pepper. Brown on all sides. Place it on its back and cook for 25 minutes in the oven.

Remove the duck from the oven, cut into four pieces, and put on a serving dish. Discard the fat from the pan, add 1 cup of cold water, and cook to reduce this juice by half, scraping the pan to loosen the juices.

Dilute the cornstarch in about 4 ounces of water. Reheat the honey mixture and add the diluted cornstarch and the reduced duck juices. Whisk until it boils, then cook for 2 minutes over low heat and whisk in the butter. Add salt and the remaining Maniguette pepper and coat the duck pieces with the sauce. Serve immediately.

CHEF'S COMMENTS: In the seventeenth century, Maniguette (or seeds of paradise) was the substitute pepper of Africans, who did not have the right to use real pepper, which was harvested and exported by the colonial power. You must mill this pepper at the last minute, as its aroma evaporates quickly.

You can do a version of this with chicken.—**TRANS.**

Duck legs braised with tea and cinnamon
Cuisses de canard confites au thé et à la cannelle

SERVES 4 | PREPARATION: 15 minutes
COOKING: 1 hour

- 4 duck legs, totaling 2 pounds (800 g), fat removed
- 1 onion
- 1 carrot
- 1 leek
- 4 tablespoons smoked green tea (tarry souchong)
- 4 sticks cinnamon
- 3 tablespoons (1½ oz, 30 g) butter
- ½ teaspoon cornstarch
- Gros sel and fine salt

Peel and wash the vegetables. Put the duck legs in a pan with the vegetables, the tea, and the cinnamon. Cover with water and season with gros sel. Cook for 1 hour, then drain. Put the legs in a serving dish.

Filter about 1 cup (20 cl) of the cooking juice into another pan, removing as much fat as possible. Dilute the cornstarch in 4 tablespoons water and whisk into the juice. Whisk in the butter, cut into pieces. Coat the duck legs with the sauce. You can sprinkle on a few tea leaves from the cooking as decoration.

You can cook this dish the day before and reheat it gently in a pan with a little oil, turning the legs after 5 minutes.

CHEF'S COMMENTS: A reverse *confit de canard*. Rather than adding fat, the tea dissolves it.

This is easy and a winner. Every time we serve the dish, it is praised. It is useful to be able to cook it in advance. We usually ask the butcher to "disarticulate" the duck legs—partially separate them into the thigh and the drumstick—to make serving easier.—**TRANS.**

Grilled chicken breasts with ginger
Blancs de volaille grillés au gingembre

SERVES 4	PREPARATION: 5 minutes COOKING: 10 minutes MARINATING: 3 to 4 hours

2 pounds (800 g) boneless, skinless chicken breasts
Juice of ½ lemon
1-inch (2.5 cm) piece of fresh ginger, grated
3 tablespoons soy sauce
1 teaspoon sugar
3 tablespoons sake or dry sherry (optional)

In a large bowl, mix together the ginger with the soy sauce, wine, sugar, and lemon juice. Add the chicken breasts and marinate for 3 to 4 hours in the refrigerator, turning them from time to time.

On a cast-iron grill or a barbecue, cook the chicken breasts for 5 minutes on each side. Don't let them get dry. Serve immediately.

CHEF'S COMMENTS: This is a simplified version of the famous Japanese yakitori brochettes. The Japanese alternate the pieces of chicken on the skewers with slices of the white of leeks. This is an excellent addition. You can grill the leeks with the chicken.

You can use a parsley grinder or a garlic press for the ginger. This recipe can also be used for fish, veal, or other meat.—**TRANS.**

Spiced guinea fowl stew
Fricassée de pintade aux six épices

SERVES 4

PREPARATION: 30 minutes
COOKING: 60 minutes

1 free-range guinea fowl cut into 8 pieces
4 cloves garlic, unpeeled
1 large onion, chopped
1 lime
½ teaspoon paprika
½ teaspoon powdered cumin
½ teaspoon powdered coriander
5 cloves
¾ ounce (20 g) fresh ginger, about a 1½-inch piece, finely grated
1 stick cinnamon
2 cups (50 cl) dry white wine
10 black olives (stones in, from Nice, if possible)
1 tablespoon cornstarch
3 tablespoons (5 cl) olive oil
Gros sel, sugar, fine salt, freshly ground pepper

Put the lime in a small pan of water, bring to a boil for 2 minutes, and discard the water. Do this two more times.

In a large, heavy-bottom pan, heat the olive oil and gently brown the guinea fowl pieces. Add the onion and cook for 2 minutes, stirring with a wooden spoon. Add all the spices, the garlic, and a pinch of sugar. Cook for 5 minutes, taking care the mixture does not stick. Add the white wine and 2 cups (50 cl) of water.

→

Cut the lime in two, then in small half-moon slices. Add these, along with the onions, to the guinea fowl. Cook for 45 minutes. (If you don't have a free-range bird the cooking time will be shorter.)

Mix the cornstarch with 4 tablespoons of water. Pour into the pan, stirring well. Let simmer for 5 minutes, add salt and pepper, and serve.

CHEF'S COMMENTS: Here is a dish halfway between the French countryside and Asia. You can adapt this recipe with other spices. Experiment!

Another great dish, which we vary a lot. Save the leftover stock for tomorrow's soup. It often makes a jellied soup. Guinea fowl needs to be stewed unless cut into thin steaks for grilling. This dish is less interesting, but possible, with red wine instead of white.—**TRANS.**

Poached chicken with black cardamom
Poularde pochée à la cardamome noire

SERVES 4 | PREPARATION: 15 minutes
COOKING: 1 hour 45 minutes

1 fattened hen ready to cook (or a large free-range chicken)
Juice of ½ lemon
1 leek
2 carrots
1 stalk celery
1 onion
1 sprig thyme
3 bay leaves
10 black cardamom pods (or if not available substitute white or green cardamom)
1⅛ cup (30 cl) crème fraîche
4 tablespoons (2 oz, 50 g) butter
Gros sel, salt, freshly ground pepper

Put the chicken in a large pot. Peel, wash, and chop coarsely the carrots, leek, onion, and celery. Put the vegetables in the pot with the thyme and bay leaf, add the cardamom pods and a pinch of gros sel. Cover with water, bring to a boil, and cook for 1 hour 45 minutes at a slow boil (a free-range chicken might need only 1 hour). Stick the point of a knife in at the top of the thigh to see if the chicken is tender; there should not be much resistance.

When the chicken is cooked, save 1⅛ cups (30 cl) bouillon and reduce it with the cardamom pods to 3 tablespoons. Add the crème fraîche and reduce for 5 minutes. Add salt, pepper, →

and the lemon juice. Bring to a boil and whisk in the butter, cut into small pieces.

Cut the chicken and serve coated with the sauce.

CHEF'S COMMENTS: You can cook the chicken the day before and keep it in the refrigerator in its juice. The infusion of spices will give it a more pronounced taste. Don't throw away the extra cooking juice; you can cook rice in it, or make a marvelous Chinese soup. Cardamom, especially black cardamom, is a spice little used in France. It should be better known, as its taste, of pepper and lemon, more earthy than that of green cardamom, is very subtle.

Excellent, but we tend to leave out the butter.—**TRANS.**

Chicken curry
Poulet au cari

SERVES 4	PREPARATION: 30 minutes COOKING: 45 minutes

1 free-range chicken cut into 8 pieces
1 onion, chopped
1 clove garlic
3½ cups (12 oz, 350 g) grated unsweetened coconut
1 bulb lemongrass, sliced
⅔ ounce (20 g) fresh ginger, about a 1½-inch piece, grated
2 tablespoons Madras curry powder
1 stick cinnamon
2 cloves
1 star anise
3 tablespoons (5 cl) peanut oil
Fine salt

Put the coconut in a pan with 2 cups (50 cl) of water. Boil for 2 minutes. Blend this liquid in three batches. Put through a fine sieve, pressing to get the maximum coconut milk.

Heat the oil in a heavy-bottom pan. Brown the chicken for 5 minutes. Add the onion, garlic. and all the spices. Cook, stirring, for 1 minute, then add the coconut milk and salt. Cook gently for 40 minutes, uncovered. (The cooking time will vary according to the quality of your chicken.)

CHEF'S COMMENTS: This is an adaptation of a Southeast Asian curry, but less spicy. Curries have always fascinated me. In Asia each family has its recipe, always different and unexpected. →

Curry is better reheated, so I suggest preparing it a day in advance and reheating it gently so as to not recook it. You can sprinkle cilantro on the curry just before serving, to add to the flavor.

We lazily use coconut powder or canned coconut sometimes. (Be sure to get unsweetened coconut.) The interest here is the mixture of star anise with curry.—**TRANS.**

Spiced chicken stew

Fricassée de volaille à la torréfaction d'épices

SERVES 4	PREPARATION: 30 minutes COOKING: 45 minutes

1 free-range chicken, cut into pieces
1 onion
1 stalk celery
1 carrot
½ teaspoon Szechuan pepper (if not available, substitute cardamom)
½ teaspoon cumin seed
½ teaspoon coriander seed
½ teaspoon mustard seed
1 tablespoon flour
6 tablespoons (10 cl) dry white wine
3 tablespoons (2 oz, 50 g) crème fraîche
3 tablespoons (5 cl) peanut oil
Juice of ½ lemon
Fine salt

Salt the chicken. Brown in oil in a frying pan or heavy pot.

Peel and wash the onion, carrot, and celery. Cut into ½-inch (1 cm) dice and add to pan with the chicken. Cook for 2 minutes, stirring with a spatula. Sprinkle with flour, add the wine and 2 cups (50 cl) of water. Cook for 40 minutes, covered, over low heat.

In another cast-iron pan, toast the spices until they take on a light color. Crush in a coffee mill.

Put the chicken on a serving dish. Add the crème fraîche →

and the spices to the pan the chicken was cooked in and let simmer for 5 minutes. Then add the lemon juice and cook another minute. Put the sauce through a fine sieve and coat the chicken. Serve immediately.

CHEF'S COMMENTS: When you turn on the coffee mill to grind the spices, their flavors will fill your kitchen.

You could omit the butter. If you don't have a coffee mill, you could use a blender.—**TRANS.**

Spiced chicken "Florence"
Poulet "Florence" aux épices

SERVES 4

PREPARATION: 10 minutes
COOKING: 40 minutes

- 1 free-range chicken
- 1 bunch spring onions
- 1 clove garlic, grated
- 1 bunch cilantro
- 2 pieces of fresh ginger the size of a walnut, peeled
- 6 tablespoons (10 cl) soy sauce
- 3 tablespoons (5 cl) peanut oil
- Gros sel

Use a wok with a cover for this recipe. Put the chicken, thigh side down, in the wok. Add 4 cups (1 liter) of cold water, a pinch of gros sel, 1 piece of ginger cut into slices, and half the cilantro. Cover and cook slowly for 20 minutes, basting frequently. Turn the chicken over, add water as needed to keep the same volume, and cook for 20 more minutes. Take out the chicken and cut it into small pieces without deboning. It should be pink.

Separate the white from the green of the spring onions. Wash the green and mince finely. Peel the bulbs and cut them into thin slices. Brown them in oil, then drain on a paper towel.

Grate the remaining ginger and cook it with the garlic for 10 seconds in the remaining oil. Add the soy sauce and 6 tablespoons of water. Then add the green of the onions. Set aside.

Put the pieces of chicken in a deep dish, coat with the sauce and, sprinkle with sprigs of cilantro. Serve with rice. →

CHEF'S COMMENTS: This is a dish I love and that a Chinese friend often makes for me. You must suck the bones to get all the flavor of the chicken.

It is more common to see spring onions—small- to medium-size balls of onions with their green attached—in France than in the United States. This dish probably began with Chinese green onions, what Americans often call scallions. Small leeks would also do. We always have fried red onions, available at any Asian shop, to use with such dishes. This can be added to other dishes for an interesting touch.—**TRANS.**

8 Vegetable Dishes

Spiced caramelized vegetables
Légumes caramélisés aux épices

SERVES 4	PREPARATION: 20 minutes COOKING: 30 minutes

4 carrots
2 bulbs fennel
4 potatoes
½ bulb celery root
4 new turnips
Juice of ½ lemon
1 stick cinnamon
3 star anise
½ teaspoon garam masala
½ teaspoon brown sugar or molasses
½ teaspoon olive oil
1½ tablespoons (¾ oz, 20 g) butter
Pinch of fleur de sel

Peel the carrots, potatoes and turnips. Trim the fennel and cut each bulb into four pieces. Peel the celery root with a knife and cut into 1-inch (2 cm) strips. Dry all the vegetables in a paper towel.

Heat the oil in a large pan, add the star anise and cinnamon, and brown for 1 minute. Add the vegetables and brown them lightly. Sprinkle with the garam masala, brown sugar, and fleur de sel. Add 1⅛ cups (30 cl) water and the butter. Cover with aluminum foil and cook for 20 minutes over low heat.

With the point of a knife, check that the vegetables are tender, then add the lemon juice and caramelize for 1 minute. There should be no more water in the pan. If the vegetables are not cooked, or if you like them very tender, add 6 tablespoons (10 cl) of water and simmer for 10 minutes longer, being sure that the water doesn't evaporate too fast. Serve immediately.

CHEF'S COMMENTS: This is vegetables as a main dish, enhanced with Indian spices. For hungry guests, you can have a risotto as a garnish. If these vegetables are not in season, you can use others. Don't hesitate to personalize this dish by choosing your favorite spices.

Vegetable couscous with a spicy vinaigrette
Couscous 100% légumes, vinaigrette d'épices

SERVES 4 | PREPARATION: 40 minutes
COOKING: 30 minutes

1 cauliflower
2 red bell peppers
2 bulbs fennel
2 eggplants
1 lime
½ cup (2 oz, 50 g) chopped almonds
1 tablespoon ras-el-hanout (or powdered cumin, or coriander)
½ teaspoon mustard seeds
½ teaspoon coriander seeds
½ teaspoon cumin seeds
½ teaspoon fenugreek seeds
¾ cup (20 cl) olive oil
2 tablespoons (1 oz, 30 g) butter

Preheat the oven to 350°F (170°).

Separate the cauliflower into pieces and cut into 1-inch (2 cm) pieces. Blend in four batches to obtain a consistency like couscous, or semolina.

In a large pan, bring some salted water to boil. Add the cauliflower. When the water boils again, cook for 30 seconds, then drain in a sieve. Set aside, continuing to drain.

Peel the red peppers with a vegetable peeler (as you would potatoes) and cut into strips 1 inch wide (2 cm) and 2 inches (4 cm) long. Cut the fennel and eggplants in ½-inch (1 cm) slices.

In a small pan, bring a little water to boil and add the spices. Boil for 1 minute, then drain.

Squeeze the lime into a bowl and add the spices, the chopped almonds, and half the olive oil.

In a large frying pan, brown the vegetables for 5 minutes with the rest of the olive oil over low heat. Put them in an ovenproof dish and finish cooking for 15 minutes in the oven.

In the frying pan, melt the butter and add the cauliflower semolina and the ras-el-hanout. Add salt and mix well for 2 minutes over low heat. Put into a serving dish and add the vegetables. Serve the sauce on the side.

CHEF'S COMMENTS: Cauliflower semolina is very tasty and goes well with the complex flavor of the ras-el-hanout. This substitute for couscous is simple to make and surprisingly light.

Having always skinned peppers by other, more complicated techniques, we did not believe they could be peeled like any other vegetable until we tried it.—**TRANS.**

Risotto of chestnuts and mushrooms with nutmeg
Risotto aux châtaignes et cèpes, parfum de muscade

SERVES 4 | PREPARATION: 15 minutes
COOKING: 25 minutes

- 1½ cups (10 oz, 300 g) Thai perfumed rice or round Italian rice
- 2¼ cups (60 cl) bouillon or chicken stock
- ¾ pound (300 g) mushrooms (cèpes, porcini, or any flavorful brown mushroom)—use more if you wish
- ¼ pound (100 g) cooked, unsweetened chestnuts, chopped
- 1 onion, finely sliced
- 1 nutmeg
- ½ cup white wine
- 3 tablespoons (5 cl) crème fraîche
- 1 tablespoon olive oil
- Salt

In a large pan, sweat the onion in the olive oil without coloring. Add the rice and cook 30 seconds, add the white wine and let it reduce. Add the bouillon. Simmer for 25 minutes, stirring frequently. When the rice is cooked it should have a creamy consistency; if it is too compact, add a little bouillon.

Scrape the cèpes, rinse if necessary, and dry on a paper towel. Cut them into ½-inch (1 cm) dice and add to the risotto. Gently mix in the crème fraîche, add salt and a little grated nutmeg.

Add more nutmeg to taste. Sprinkle the chestnuts over the risotto and mix gently. Serve hot.

CHEF'S COMMENTS: Nutmeg adds a foreign touch to this autumn dish. Accompany with a salad.

To control the texture, add the bouillon in several stages so it is mostly absorbed before you add more liquid.—**TRANS.**

Tomato tart with poppy seeds
Tarte de tomates au pavot

SERVES 4	PREPARATION: 45 minutes COOKING: 15 minutes REFRIGERATION: 10 minutes

1¼ pounds (500 g) puff pastry
8 firm red tomatoes
10 tablespoons (1½ oz, 40 g) poppy seeds
½ cup (2 oz, 50 g) flour
6 tablespoons (10 cl) olive oil
Gros sel

Preheat the oven to 400°F (200°C).

Divide the puff pastry in two, flour both halves, and roll out to make two rounds 12 inches (30 cm) in diameter. Put in the refrigerator, flat.

Fill a pan halfway with water and bring to a boil. Have a bowl of very cold water ready. With the point of a knife, remove the stalks of the tomatoes before plunging them into boiling water for 10 seconds. Remove them and plunge immediately into the cold water. Peel and cut in four pieces. Remove the seeds and squeeze to juice so that just the flesh remains. Salt all the pieces and put in the refrigerator for 10 minutes.

Drain the tomatoes on a paper towel, then place the pieces in a rosette pattern on the puff pastry. Add gros sel and sprinkle with poppy seeds. Cook in the oven for 15 minutes. If your oven is not large enough for 2 tarts at the same time, prepare only one, so the other does not get soggy. Moisten with olive oil when the tarts come out of the oven. Serve hot.

CHEF'S COMMENTS: The simplicity of the poppy seeds enhances this tart, one of my favorites. Accompany it with a rather bitter salad (rocket, curly endive, etc.).

You can use frozen puff pastry.—**TRANS.**

Cabbage stuffed with eggplant, sweet potato, and caraway seeds

Chou farci d'aubergine et de patate douce au carvi

SERVES 4

PREPARATION: 40 minutes
COOKING: 25 minutes

- 1 green cabbage
- 4 eggplants, cut in half lengthwise
- 2 sweet potatoes (1 pound [400 g] total), peeled and cut into ½-inch (1 cm) dice
- ½ cup (2 oz, 50 g) walnut halves
- 1 tablespoon caraway seeds
- 6 tablespoons (10 cl) olive oil
- Gros sel, fine salt

Preheat the oven to 350°F (180°C)

Separate the cabbage leaves, saving 8 large ones and chopping the others finely.

Put the eggplant pieces in an ovenproof dish, salt, moisten with olive oil, and cook for 30 minutes in the oven. Let them cool. Lower the oven temperature to 300°F (150°C).

Chop the nuts coarsely; blanch them for 1 minute in a small pan of boiling water and drain.

Have a bowl of ice water ready. Bring a large pan of water with gros sel to boil, blanch the 8 large cabbage leaves for 30 seconds, then plunge immediately into the ice water. Repeat this procedure with the strips of cabbage, blanching for 1 minute. Drain all the cabbage, pressing it with your hands to remove as much water as you can.

In a large frying pan, heat the remaining olive oil and brown the sweet potato and the caraway seeds. Add salt.

Scrape the flesh of the cooked eggplants with a spoon and add it to the sweet potatoes. Add the nuts and the strips of cabbage. Heat this mixture, stirring well. Add salt.

Spread out 2 of the cabbage leaves to get a round surface on which you put one quarter of the vegetable mixture. Close well, pressing the upper leaf. Repeat this for the other cabbage leaves and then cook them for 15 minutes in the oven, taking care to cover with aluminum foil to avoid their drying out. Serve accompanied with curried vinaigrette with red beets (p. 217).

CHEF'S COMMENTS: The lightly anise flavor of caraway seeds goes very well with cabbage.

This would not seem complicated to your grandmother, who probably also made stuffed cabbage dishes.—**TRANS.**

Spinach au gratin with pumpkin and coriander
Gratin d'épinards au potiron et à la coriandre

SERVES 4	PREPARATION: 45 minutes COOKING: 40 minutes

- 2¼ pounds (1 kg) pumpkin
- 2¼ pounds (1 kg) spinach
- 18 ounces (500 g) sorrel
- 1 tablespoon powdered coriander (or cumin)
- 1 nutmeg
- 2½ cups (9 oz, 250 g) grated cheese (beaufort, ideally, or gruyère)
- 4 tablespoons butter
- Salt

Preheat the oven to 350°F (180°C).

Peel the pumpkin and cut it into strips 1 inch (2 cm) thick. Cook the strips for 8 minutes in the microwave. Drain in a sieve.

Clean the spinach and sorrel and remove the stems. Dry it as for a salad. In a large frying pan, heat half the butter. Add half the spinach and sorrel with salt and a little grated nutmeg. Cook for 2 minutes, then remove. Repeat for the other half. If your pan is small, you can repeat this procedure several times.

Put the pumpkin in a gratin dish. Add salt and coriander and half the cheese. Cover with the spinach-sorrel mixture and then another layer of cheese. Cook for 25 minutes in the top of the oven to brown the top.

CHEF'S COMMENTS: Coriander links the sweetness of the pumpkin with the acidity of the sorrel.

The recipe calls for the larger pumpkin, which could be replaced by a squash if not too sweet.—**TRANS.**

9 Vegetables as Garnish

Celeriac (celery root) with fennel seed

Céleri-rave aux graines de fenouil

SERVES 4 | PREPARATION: 20 minutes; COOKING: 30 minutes

- 1 large bulb celeriac
- 1 lemon cut in half
- 1 tablespoon fennel seeds
- ¼ teaspoon turmeric
- 2 cups (50 cl) chicken stock (or use water with an onion cut in quarters)
- ¾ cup (20 cl) whipping (heavy) cream
- Salt, freshly ground pepper

Peel the celeriac with a knife, being careful not to cut into the root too deeply. Wash and dry the root and rub with half the lemon. Squeeze the other half lemon.

Cut the celeriac into ⅛-inch (2 mm) slices. Then cut the slices into sticks of the same thickness. Put the sticks on a cutting board and cut into ⅛-inch (2 mm) dice.

In a pan, combine the celeriac, fennel seeds, chicken stock, and lemon juice. Bring to a boil and cook until all the liquid has evaporated. (Remove the onion if you used one.) Add the cream and turmeric and cook until thick. Add salt and pepper and serve hot.

CHEF'S COMMENTS: In this flavorful garnish, the slight anise taste of the fennel seeds goes well with the celeriac. If you don't have fennel seeds, you could use cumin, caraway, or dill seeds. Use it to accompany a white meat or a baked fish.

Celeriac is more common in Europe than in the United States. It cooks in liquid easily and need not be cut into such small pieces. We love it pureed.—**TRANS.**

Browned rice with cumin

Riz grillé au cumin

SERVES 4

PREPARATION: 5 minutes
COOKING: 40 minutes
RESTING TIME: 10 minutes

1 cup (7 oz, 200 g) Thai rice
1 tablespoon powdered cumin
6 tablespoons (3 oz, 75 g) butter
Fine salt

Put the rice in a pan. Add water to cover and go to the level of the second joint of your index finger. Add a pinch of salt, bring to a boil, lower the heat, cover, and cook 20 to 25 minutes over low heat. When the rice is cooked, remove from heat and let it puff up for 10 minutes. Mix the cumin powder with the rice. Add salt if needed.

Heat the butter in a nonstick pan. Add the rice and cook for 15 minutes on a low heat, taking care not to burn the rice. Place a shallow dish upside down on the pan, and carefully turn the pan over so that the rice falls in one piece on the serving dish, browned side up.

CHEF'S COMMENTS: In Asia there are hundreds of ways of using rice. I got this recipe from an Indian; it is a treat. For any rice dish, you get the best results cooking a large quantity. I think 1 cup of uncooked rice is the minimum. This can accompany almost all dishes with sauce. Use your imagination.

An original way to measure the amount of water!—**TRANS.**

Tomatoes with poppy seeds
Tomates panées aux graines de pavot

SERVES 4	PREPARATION: 20 minutes COOKING: 10 minutes

8 ripe tomatoes
4 salted anchovy fillets
2 tablespoons poppy seeds
3 tablespoons (5 cl) olive oil
4 tablespoons (2 oz, 50 g) lightly softened butter
Salt, freshly ground pepper

Preheat the oven to 150°F (60°C).

Fill a large pan halfway with water and bring to a boil. Remove the stem and hard core from the tomatoes with a knife. Have a bowl of very cold water ready (add ice cubes if you want). Plunge the tomatoes into the boiling water for 10 seconds. Remove and plunge immediately into the cold water. Peel the tomatoes and cut in two horizontally. Take out the seeds with a small spoon and put the tomatoes on a paper towel to drain as much water as possible. Set aside.

In the blender, puree the anchovies and butter.

Put the tomatoes on an ovenproof sheet and sprinkle with olive oil, salt, and pepper. Put a spoonful of butter on each tomato and dust with poppy seeds. Cook for 10 minutes in the oven. Remove them with a slotted spatula to eliminate the water from the tomatoes. →

CHEF'S COMMENTS: This is a tasty variation on the tomato-anchovy combination, with the crunchy addition of poppy seeds. Use it to accompany sautéed or poached fish, which go well with the acidity of the tomatoes.

Save the tomato juice when seeding. It can be used to drink, for sauce, for soup, etc.—**TRANS.**

Spinach with nutmeg
Épinards fondus à la noix de muscade

SERVES 4	PREPARATION: 20 minutes COOKING: 2 minutes

2¼ pounds (1 kg) fresh spinach, stems removed
1 nutmeg
2 tablespoons (1 oz, 20 g) butter
Salt, freshly ground pepper

Wash the spinach three times. Dry as for a salad.

In a large pan, heat the butter, add the spinach, cover, and cook over medium heat for 1 minute, stirring often. Grate a bit of nutmeg on the spinach, add a pinch of salt and one turn of the pepper mill. When the spinach has wilted, press it with a spatula on the side of the pan to remove as much water as possible.

CHEF'S COMMENTS: Butter and nutmeg: everyone knows this seasoning for spinach. You can also add a little finely grated orange rind. Use this to accompany a white meat, a poached fish, or a chicken.

French cooks sauté spinach for a short time, so it is more wilted than cooked. You can add lemon, garlic, caraway seeds, or tomato cubes. We boil the stems with other discarded parts of vegetables to make bouillon or soup. A chef should find a use for everything.—**TRANS.**

Spiced carrot mousse
Mousse de carotte aux épices

SERVES 4	PREPARATION: 20 minutes COOKING: 20 minutes

2¼ pounds (1 kg) carrots, cut into 1-inch (2 cm) rounds
6 tablespoons (4 oz, 100 g) thick crème fraîche
½ teaspoon curry powder
½ teaspoon powdered cumin
Salt, freshly ground white pepper

Cook the carrots for 20 minutes in salted water. Remove when they are tender but not mushy. (If they are too hard, the puree will be grainy; if too soft, it will be liquid.)

In a pan, bring the crème fraîche and the spices to a boil. Blend the carrots to get a smooth puree, and whisk in the cream and spices. Check the seasoning.

CHEF'S COMMENTS: The carrots are enhanced by the curry. This puree can be served hot or cold. Use it to accompany a baked or poached fish, or white meat.

You can do something similar with other vegetables such as eggplant or celeriac.—**TRANS.**

Curried fettuccine

Fetticcine au cari

SERVES 2	PREPARATION: 10 minutes COOKING: 3 minutes

5 ounces (150 g) fresh fettuccine
Grated zest of ½ lemon
½ teaspoon curry powder
1½ tablespoons (1 oz, 25 g) thick crème fraîche
Gros sel, fine salt, freshly ground pepper

In a large pan, boil water with gros sel. Add the fettuccine and cook for 3 minutes. Put in a sieve and refresh under cold running water to stop the cooking. Drain.

Put the crème fraîche, curry powder, lemon zest, and a pinch of salt in a pan. Bring to a boil while whisking. Add the pasta. Cook for 1 minute over very low heat. Check the seasoning and serve immediately.

CHEF'S COMMENTS: Curry adds aroma to this simple preparation. The lemon zest gives a lively touch to the cream. If you double the proportions you will have a main-course dish for two. Use this to accompany all the stews and meats in sauce.

Remember to use lemon zest in other pasta sauces.—**TRANS.**

Spiced eggplant

Aubergines confites aux épices douces

SERVES 4	PREPARATION: 20 minutes COOKING: 30 minutes

- 2¼ pounds (1 kg) eggplants, peeled and cut into ½-inch (1 cm) dice
- 1 large onion, finely chopped
- ¼ teaspoon powdered coriander
- ¼ teaspoon powdered cumin
- ½ teaspoon curry powder
- 2 cups (50 cl) milk
- 1 cup (25 cl) whipping (heavy) cream
- 3 tablespoons (5 cl) olive oil
- Salt, freshly ground pepper

Pour the olive oil in a large pan, add the onion, and cook for 1 minute without browning. Add all the spices and stir with a wooden spoon for 1 minute. Add the eggplants and milk. Salt lightly, bring to a boil, and mix well. Cook for 15 minutes at a slow boil. The eggplants should melt between your fingers when done. Put the mixture in a sieve and drain for 2 minutes, stirring from time to time.

When the eggplants have been drained, pour the cream in the pan and reduce for 1 minute. Then add the drained eggplants and simmer for 10 minutes, stirring from time to time so the mixture does not stick. Add salt and pepper to taste.

CHEF'S COMMENTS: This dish is inspired by Indian cooking, which often uses milk. Use this to accompany fish, which goes particularly well with the eggplant, or serve with roasted meats.

In this and some other recipes the goal is to cook the eggplant to a soft mash. The same idea works for eggplant as a sauce for pasta, stewed with chicken, etc.—**TRANS.**

Curried green lentils
Lentilles vertes étuvées au cari

SERVES 4	PREPARATION: 20 minutes COOKING: 35 minutes

8 ounces (200 g) green lentils
2 ounces (50 g) smoked bacon, cut into 4 pieces
1 carrot
1 onion
1 bay leaf
1 sprig thyme
1 clove
½ stick cinnamon
½ teaspoon curry powder
6 tablespoons (10 cl) crème fraîche
Gros sel, fine salt, freshly ground pepper

Wash the lentils in cold water two or three times. Peel and quarter the onion, and put the clove in one of the quarters. Peel and slice the carrot. Cut the bacon in 4 pieces.

Put all these ingredients with the lentils in a medium-size pan. Add the thyme, bay leaf, and cinnamon. Cover with water and simmer for 25 minutes. Do not overcook the lentils. When they are cooked, add a pinch of gros sel.

Remove the spices. Drain the lentils, keeping a bit of the juice. Add the crème fraîche and the curry powder. Simmer for 5 more minutes over low heat. Add salt and pepper to taste. Serve hot.

CHEF'S COMMENTS: Indians know the combination of lentils and curry well, but they make it much hotter than in this recipe. Use this to accompany pork or lamb.

Those who are not fans of smoked bacon might use chicken bouillon instead.—**TRANS.**

Cauliflower cake with turmeric
Gâteau de chou-fleur au curcuma

SERVES 4	PREPARATION: 20 minutes COOKING: 1 hour 40 minutes REFRIGERATION: 12 hours

18 ounces (500 g) cauliflower
2 eggs
½ teaspoon turmeric
¾ cup (8 oz, 200 g) thick crème fraîche
4 tablespoons (2 oz, 50 g) butter
Salt

Preheat the oven to 350°F (180°C).

Wash the cauliflower and divide into florets. Cook in a steamer for 10 minutes; it should remain crunchy.

In a large bowl, combine the cauliflower, crème fraîche, turmeric, and eggs. Whisk until the cauliflower is broken into small pieces. Add salt.

Line a terrine dish with buttered aluminum foil. Add the cauliflower mixture. Cover the dish and bake for 1 hour in a bain-marie. Then remove the lid and cook for 30 minutes more. Let cool, then refrigerate for 12 hours.

About 20 minutes before serving, remove the terrine from the refrigerator. Put a knife point between the aluminum and the dish, pull on the paper from both sides, and reverse the terrine on a board. Remove the paper and cut the terrine in 1-inch (2 cm) slices.

In a nonstick pan, melt 2 tablespoons (30 g) of butter. When it is hot, place the slices of terrine in the pan and brown them, gently, for 2 minutes on each side. Be careful, as the slices are fragile.

CHEF'S COMMENTS: Turmeric adds a sweet flavor, rather like nutmeg, and also a nice golden color. Use this to accompany a roast pork or veal, a shoulder or leg of lamb.

The idea of cooked vegetables with eggs and cream can be applied to other dishes, including tarts with eggplant, carrots, sweet potatoes, and spinach.—**TRANS.**

Potato cakes with tonka beans and buckwheat
Galettes parmentières à la fève tonka et au sarrasin

SERVES 4	PREPARATION: 20 minutes COOKING: 30 minutes REFRIGERATION: 12 hours

18 ounces (500 g) potatoes (Charlottes or new potatoes)
3 egg yolks
Pinch of tonka bean (or powdered cumin)
3 tablespoons thick crème fraîche
3 tablespoons buckwheat flour
Salt

Peel and wash the potatoes, and cut in large pieces. Rinse them under running water. Cook in lightly salted water, drain, and puree.

Add to the potato puree the crème fraîche, then the egg yolks, one by one, and finally the buckwheat flour. Stir well after adding each egg yolk so it does not coagulate on contact with the hot puree. Check the seasoning, adding salt to taste.

Grate the tonka bean on top of the puree, bit by bit, checking the taste, as the tonka bean is quite powerful. You can use this preparation right away, but it is easier to mold if you refrigerate it for 12 hours.

Place cakes, each made from about 1 tablespoon of puree, in a nonstick frying pan or pancake griddle about 12 inches (32 cm) in diameter. Do not use fat. Prepare 5 or 6 cakes at a time. Put the pan over low heat and cook until well browned. Turn over with a plastic spatula and cook the other side for 2 to 3 minutes. Serve immediately as a garnish.

CHEF'S COMMENTS: Makers of perfume use the tonka bean to charm the nose. Here you will be able to taste the flavor. This can accompany red meat, but potatoes go well with many dishes. Try different combinations.

If adding herbs, olives, or sweet peppers, avoid overdoing it as the potato taste should predominate. Be careful with the tonka bean, which is poisonous in large quantities.—**TRANS.**

Belgian endives with orange, ginger, and coriander
Endives à l'orange, au gingembre, et à la coriandre

SERVES 4

PREPARATION: 15 minutes
COOKING: 45 minutes

- 4 endives
- Juice of 4 oranges
- Juice of ½ lemon
- ¾ ounce (20 g) fresh ginger, about a 1½-inch piece, finely grated
- 1 tablespoon coriander seeds
- 4 tablespoons (2 oz, 50 g) butter, cut into small pieces
- 1 tablespoon sugar
- Fine salt

Preheat the oven to 350°F (180°C).

Take the base and any bad leaves off the endives and cut in half lengthwise. Put in an ovenproof dish and cover with the orange and lemon juice. Sprinkle the endives with the sugar, a little salt, coriander, ginger, and the butter. Cover with aluminum foil and cook for 45 minutes. The endives should be very tender.

Remove the foil and put the dish under the broiler for a few seconds to brown. Serve immediately.

CHEF'S COMMENTS: The flavor of coriander seeds, as you bite into them, goes very well with endive. You could cook the endives a day in advance and reheat in a pot with a little butter just before serving. Traditionally, endives are cooked with lemon. Lime is also possible. Here there are interesting contrasts. Use this to accompany white meat and fish, or serve it as a main course for real vegetable lovers!

Again, spice seeds are used for contrasting texture. Caraway or poppy seeds might be possible.—**TRANS.**

Mashed potatoes with tonka beans
Pomme de terre écrasée à la fève tonka

SERVES 4	PREPARATION: 15 minutes COOKING: 15 minutes REFRIGERATION: 12 hours

18 ounces (500 g) potatoes (Charlottes or new potatoes)
1 tonka bean (or substitute 1 nutmeg)
1 tablespoon olive oil
1 tablespoon peanut oil
Salt

Wash and brush the potatoes and cook in their skins in salted water. Check them with a knife point; do not overcook. Refrigerate for 12 hours (the starch will loosen, which will keep the potatoes from being too sticky when they are mashed).

The next day, peel the potatoes and mash them with a fork in a heavy-bottom pan. Grate a little tonka bean with a nutmeg grater, then add the two oils and a little more tonka bean. Salt lightly and heat gently, stirring frequently so that the potatoes don't stick. Add tonka bean if you like a stronger flavor.

It is better to add the tonka bean at several intervals, tasting each time, for it is a powerful flavor that can become disagreeable if you overdo it.

CHEF'S COMMENTS: The tonka bean has a unique and incomparable flavor that goes well with many dishes. It will astonish your guests as they eat these simple potatoes. Use this to accompany any dishes of poached fish.

Other alternatives are seeded black olives and garlic cloves. Note Delacourcelle's trick of refrigerating the cooked potatoes before peeling and mashing.—**TRANS.**

Pumpkin au gratin with dill seeds
Gratin de potiron à la graine d'aneth

SERVES 4	PREPARATION: 20 minutes COOKING: 20 minutes

- 2¼ pounds (1 kg) muscat pumpkin
- 1 tablespoon dill seeds
- 2 cups (50 cl) thick crème fraîche
- Salt, freshly ground pepper

Preheat the oven to 350°F (180°C).

Peel the pumpkin and remove all the seeds. Cut it vertically in 1½-inch (3 cm) strips, then cut these in ¼-inch (5 mm) slices.

In a small pan, heat the crème fraîche and the dill seeds. Boil gently for about 2 minutes, until the mixture thickens slightly. Add salt and pepper.

Spread the slices of pumpkin on a gratin dish, overlapping them in a spiral pattern. Moisten with the cream and cook in the oven for 20 minutes. Check the pumpkin from time to time; it should have the consistency of a boiled potato. Serve immediately.

CHEF'S COMMENTS: In France dill leaves are better known than dill seeds, which are, however, used in eastern and northern Europe. Here they bring a fresh, lively flavor to the pumpkin. Use this to accompany pork, especially grilled pork or cutlets.

Again he has in mind the large pumpkin. Some squashes will do.—**TRANS.**

Zucchini with spiced cream
Courgettes à la crème d'épices

SERVES 4

PREPARATION: 20 minutes
COOKING: 15 minutes
DRAINING: 3 hours

- 2 pounds small, firm, green zucchini
- 1 small onion, finely chopped
- 1 clove garlic, finely grated
- 1½-inch piece of fresh ginger, peeled, finely grated
- ½ teaspoon curry powder
- ¾ cup (20 cl) whipping (heavy) cream
- 1 tablespoon olive oil
- Gros sel, fine salt

Wash and lightly brush the zucchini. Remove the ends, then cut lengthwise into four pieces, then into sticks 1¼ (3 cm) inches long.

In a large pan, boil water with a large pinch of gros sel. Have a bowl of very cold water ready (use ice cubes if necessary). Cook the zucchini for 3 minutes in boiling water, then transfer to the cold water with a skimmer. Drain for at least 3 hours in a sieve.

Cook the onion gently in the olive oil in a large pan. Combine the garlic and ginger with the onion, add the curry powder, and cook for 30 seconds without browning. Add the cream and let simmer until the sauce thickens. Mix this sauce carefully with the zucchini and heat for 1 minute. Check the seasoning and serve.

CHEF'S COMMENTS: The amount of curry powder you use depends on how strong it is. You can cook the zucchini the →

day before and let it drain all night. Draining for a long time is the secret of this recipe's success. The spicy cream can also be used for other vegetables, such as broccoli, cauliflower, peas, and tarbais (white) beans. Any poached dish goes well with this recipe, but do not serve it with a dish having sauce, as the cream will not mix well with another sauce.

Red cabbage with apples and garam masala

Chou rouge aux pommes et au garam masala

SERVES 6 to 8

PREPARATION: 15 minutes
COOKING: 1 hour

- 1 red cabbage
- 4 apples
- 1 tablespoon garam masala
- 6 tablespoons (10 cl) vinegar
- 4 tablespoons (2 oz, 50 g) butter
- ½ teaspoon brown sugar
- Fine salt

Preheat the oven to 350°F (180°C).

Peel and core the apples and cut them in fine slices. Cut the cabbage in quarters, remove the hard base, and cut each quarter in three, then in 1-inch (2 cm) slices.

In a gratin dish, melt the butter, add the cabbage, and cook it gently for 5 minutes. Then add the apples and the garam masala. Cook for 5 minutes more. Add the vinegar, brown sugar, and 1⅛ cups (30 cl) water. Salt. Cover with aluminum foil and cook in the oven for 30 minutes.

Remove from the oven, stir, and cook for 30 minutes more. Check with the point of a knife to see if the cabbage is tender. If you want it more tender, add 6 tablespoons (10 cl) water and cook 15 minutes more. Check the seasoning and serve warm. →

CHEF'S COMMENTS: This dish, spiced with garam masala, can be used as a chutney, hot or cold. Surprisingly, it can accompany many dishes, from game to white meat to fish. You can keep the cabbage for several days in the refrigerator.

This is excellent, but a couple might want to make half of the recipe.—**TRANS.**

Cauliflower with caraway seeds

Poêlée de chou-fleur aux graines de carvi

SERVES 4	PREPARATION: 10 minutes COOKING: 10 minutes DRAINING: 1 hour

1 cauliflower
½ teaspoon caraway seeds (or cumin seeds)
2 tablespoons (1 oz, 30 g) butter
Gros sel, fine salt

Divide the cauliflower into florets, keeping a bit of stem, then wash and drain.

In a large pan, boil water with a pinch of gros sel. Add the cauliflower and cook 4 to 5 minutes. Check the cauliflower with the point of a knife; it should stay crunchy. Put it into cold water to stop the cooking and then drain for 1 hour in a sieve. (If you don't have time to wait, dry the cauliflower in a salad spinner, taking care to turn gently.)

Heat the butter in a frying pan, then add the cauliflower and caraway seeds. Brown the cauliflower, add salt, and serve immediately.

CHEF'S COMMENTS: Crunchy cauliflower and caraway seeds go very well together. You will be surprised by the simplicity and flavor of this recipe. It can accompany veal, pork, and all fowls; those who love vegetables can serve it by itself in a large plate!

We had old, dried caraway seeds we seldom used except for stews; then we bought good-quality seeds and we have become caraway addicts, sprinkling the seeds on salads, sautés, even sweet dishes.—**TRANS.**

Sautéed white radish with Szechuan pepper
Radis blanc daikon sauté au poivre du Sichuan

SERVES 4

PREPARATION: 20 minutes
COOKING: 15 minutes

- 2¼ pounds (1 kg) daikon white radishes (or substitute turnips)
- 1 teaspoon Szechuan pepper (ground finely in a pepper mill)
- 2 tablespoons honey
- 3 tablespoons (5 cl) peanut oil
- 1½ tablespoons (¾ oz, 20 g) butter
- Fine salt

Peel the radishes with a vegetable peeler. Wash and cut in ½-inch (1 cm) rounds.

Cook the radishes for 5 minutes in boiling water, then drain.

In a frying pan, heat half the oil and sauté half the radish rounds until lightly browned. Add 1 tablespoon honey, butter, and ½ teaspoon Szechuan pepper. Caramelize lightly, stirring frequently. Repeat this process for the remaining radishes.

CHEF'S COMMENTS: The Japanese daikon is a long, white radish, often served raw, grated in long strips, with sushi and sashimi, or cooked in bouillons and soups. For this recipe you could also cut it into ½-inch (1 cm) dice and sauté it directly without blanching, then follow the rest of the recipe. The radish is quite watery, and its taste is enhanced by the lemony and menthol taste of the Szechuan pepper.

This is an interesting way of using daikon, now often seen in supermarkets. You can use it cold the next day. If you have several pepper mills you can keep one filled with Szechuan pepper, useful for many recipes.—**TRANS.**

Pureed sweet potato and preserved ginger
Purée de patate douce au gingembre

SERVES 5 to 6

PREPARATION: 35 minutes
COOKING: 20 minutes

- 2¼ pounds (1 kg) sweet potatoes, peeled and cut into rounds or dice
- 2 lemons
- 1 cup (4 oz, 100 g) candied ginger
- 6 tablespoons (10 cl) olive oil
- 4 tablespoons thick crème fraîche
- Fine salt

Moisten the sweet potatoes with the juice of 1 lemon, mix well, and steam for 20 minutes.

In a pan, cover the second lemon with cold water, bring to a boil, and cook for 5 minutes. Throw out the water. Repeat this process three times. Then let the lemon cool and chop it in small pieces.

Cut the candied ginger into fine dice. Rinse and drain it.

Mash the sweet potatoes with a potato masher. Mix the olive oil and cream, then add to the puree. Add the lemon, ginger, and salt.

CHEF'S COMMENTS: This is even better prepared the day before; the ginger will be more pronounced. In that case, reheat, covered, for 10 minutes in the microwave. You can also serve this cold, as a condiment for a poached fish. Use this to accompany game, duck, or beef.

We like pureed sweet potato as a cold vegetable the next day.—**TRANS.**

10 Seasonings

Olive oil with sumac
Huile d'olive au sumac

PREPARATION: 5 minutes
INFUSION: 24 hours

1 cup (25 cl) olive oil
1 tablespoon powdered sumac
Fine salt

Mix all the ingredients and let them infuse for 24 hours. Pour into a 2-cup (50 cl) bottle; it will be easier to shake it, as the sumac tends to fall quickly to the bottom.

To use: This oil goes perfectly with poached fish or with vegetable salad.

Sumac, a biblical tree bark, is common to Middle Eastern cuisine and goes well with chicken and turkey, even onions.—**TRANS.**

Moroccan spiced vinaigrette
Vinaigrette au ras-el-hanout

PREPARATION: 5 minutes

2 cups (50 cl) peanut oil
5 tablespoons (8 cl) balsamic vinegar
1 tablespoon ras-el-hanout
Fine salt

Mix all the ingredients in a large bowl. Whisk well to amalgamate, then pour into a bottle.

To use: This vinaigrette can be used as a sauce if warmed. On a duck fillet or veal liver it is marvelous. Cold, it can season salads (scallops, shrimps, lobster, etc.).

This is a sort of balsamic vinaigrette with a curry flavor, a variation on the balsamic vinegar sauces French chefs have been using with fish.—**TRANS.**

Olive oil flavored with ginger juice

Huile d'olive au jus de gingembre

PREPARATION: 5 minutes

2 cups (50 cl) olive oil
1½ cups (12 oz, 300 g) fresh ginger
Fine salt

Grate the ginger and press the pulp in your hand to extract the juice (you should have about 6 tablespoons [10 cl]). Put the juice through a fine sieve.

Add the olive oil and salt. Put into a bottle, then refrigerate. Shake well before using.

To use: This seasoning is particularly delicious with avocados. It also goes well with poached fish and vegetable salads.

Thais marinate fish and fowl with ginger. You could use a garlic press to squeeze the ginger.—**TRANS.**

Olive oil with anise-flavored spices

Huile d'olive aux épices anisées

PREPARATION: 5 minutes
INFUSION: 4 to 5 hours

2 cups (50 cl) olive oil
2 lemons
2 star anise
1 tablespoon fennel seeds
1 tablespoon cumin seeds
Fine salt

Heat the oil gently with all the spices and infuse for 4 to 5 hours in a warm place. Squeeze the lemons and add the juice. Salt. Sieve and pour into a bottle.

To use: This sauce goes well with all fish. Also try it on fresh pasta or on potatoes in their jackets.

It is always useful to have such flavored oils and salts handy when cooking in a hurry and needing something to spice a dish.—**TRANS.**

Lemongrass vinaigrette

Vinaigrette à la citronnelle

PREPARATION: 5 minutes

- 2 cups (50 cl) olive oil
- 1 stalk fresh lemongrass
- Juice of 2 lemons
- Fine salt

In the blender, combine the oil, lemon juice, a pinch of salt, and the fleshy bulb of the lemongrass (about 2 inches [4 cm]). Puree for 30 seconds. Sieve and pour into a bottle. Store in the refrigerator.

To use: This sauce is best with dishes with a strong taste, such as artichokes, fennel, leeks. Another use is with fish baked in the oven.

A variation on lemon oil, this can be dribbled on any antipasto plate.—**TRANS.**

Curried vinaigrette with red beets

Vinaigrette au cari et à la betterave rouge

PREPARATION: 5 minutes

- 2½ tablespoons (2 oz, 50 g) cooked and peeled red beets
- 1⅛ cups (30 cl) peanut oil
- 6 tablespoons (10 cl) sherry vinegar
- ½ teaspoon curry powder
- Fine salt

Pour all the ingredients in a blender and puree for 15 seconds. Taste, salt if needed, and blend 2 more seconds. Sieve and pour into a bottle.

To use: This vinaigrette can be used in salads of game, terrines, or shellfish.

Beet vinaigrette has become common in Paris, but seems to us too subtle. The curry gives it some life.—**TRANS.**

Spiced seasoning for warm salads
Assaisonnement aux épices pour salade

PREPARATION: 5 minutes

1 tablespoon mustard seeds
1 tablespoon coriander seeds
½ teaspoon fenugreek seeds
1 tablespoon strong Dijon mustard
1⅛ cups (30 cl) walnut oil
9 tablespoons (15 cl) sherry vinegar
Fine salt, freshly ground pepper

Put all the spice seeds in a pan half full of water. Boil for 3 minutes, then drain.

In a bowl, whisk the mustard with the drained spices. Salt, add the vinegar little by little, then gently whisk in the oil. Check the seasoning, then pour into a bottle.

To use: This dressing is excellent with warm potatoes and other warm vegetables as salad.

Salad dressing traditionally uses 1 part vinegar to 3 or 4 parts oil. In recent years the proportions have become 1 part vinegar to 2 parts oil, which some people find too strong. You might want to taste this as you go along.—**TRANS.**

Peanut oil infused with vanilla

Huile infusée à la vanille

PREPARATION: 5 minutes
INFUSION: 1 hour

1⅛ cups (30 cl) peanut oil
Juice of 1 lemon
1 vanilla bean
Fine salt

Cut the vanilla bean in half lengthwise and remove the seeds with a knife. Put them in the oil and heat lightly for 1 minute. (Be sure not to boil.) Let them infuse for 1 hour.

When the oil comes back to room temperature, add salt and the lemon juice. Mix well and pour into a small bottle.

To use: This seasoning goes well with salads (lamb's lettuce, romaine, etc.) as well as with scallops or a cold white meat (pork, chicken, or turkey).

Although vanilla oil is commercially available, off-the-shelf oils are often flavorless. It is better to make your own.—**TRANS.**

Red pepper, apple, pear, and cumin salsa
Condiment de poivron rouge, pomme, poire, et cumin

PREPARATION: 30 minutes
COOKING: 6 minutes

For a 2¼-pound (1 kg) jar:

1⅛ pounds (500 g) red bell peppers
1 firm pear
1 Granny Smith apple
1-inch piece of fresh ginger
½ teaspoon cumin powder
1 tablespoon sugar
2 tablespoons white vinegar
Fine salt

Peel the red bell peppers with a vegetable peeler. Cut them in half and remove the seeds and the white ribs. Cut into small dice. Boil them in water for 1 minute. Set aside.

Peel and grate the ginger. Peel and seed the apple and pear. Cut them into dice.

Put the vinegar, cumin, ginger, sugar, and 4 tablespoons of water in a pan. Boil for 30 seconds, then add the red pepper and the fruit. Cook for 5 minutes over low heat, then put in a jar. Let cool uncovered, then cover the jar. Keep in the refrigerator.

To use: This salsa goes well with poached or grilled fish as well as with pork.

We do not remember when such condiments became popular, but we always have a few in the refrigerator to add to cold meats or late-night dishes or to add interest to simple grilled dishes. —**TRANS.**

Sweet potato, poppy seed, and ginger salsa
Condiment de patate douce, pivot, et gingembre

PREPARATION: 30 minutes
COOKING: 10 minutes

For a 2¼-pound (1 kg) jar:

1⅛ pounds (500 g) sweet potatoes
2 limes
1 cup (4 oz, 100 g) candied ginger
1 tablespoon poppy seeds
6 tablespoons (10 cl) olive oil
Fine salt

Peel the limes with a vegetable peeler. Cut the peel into fine dice, cover with water, and bring to a boil. Filter through a fine sieve. Repeat this procedure twice. Chop the ginger in small pieces. Squeeze one of the limes.

Peel the sweet potatoes, wash them, and cut into large dice. Steam for about 10 minutes or until tender. When they are cooked, mash them in a bowl with a fork. Add the olive oil, lime peel, poppy seeds, ginger, lime juice, and salt. Press the salsa well to remove the air. Store in the refrigerator in a jar.

To use: This salsa goes well with seafood but also with white meats. It keeps very well in the refrigerator.

Mayonnaise with toasted sesame oil
Mayonnaise à l'huile de sésame grillé

PREPARATION: 10 minutes

2 egg yolks
9 tablespoons (15 cl) peanut oil
9 tablespoons (15 cl) toasted sesame oil
1 tablespoon Dijon mustard
1 tablespoon white wine vinegar
Fine salt

Put the egg yolks, mustard, and a pinch of salt in a bowl. Whisk for 15 seconds. Add the oils very gently, whisking continually. (Don't pour too quickly, or the mayonnaise will turn.) Add the vinegar and whisk. Keep in a cool place.

To use: Serve this mayonnaise with a cold fish, such as tuna, mackerel, or hake.

Toasted sesame oil has a distinctive flavor. Look for it.—**TRANS.**

Artichoke, preserved lemons, and curry salsa
Condiment d'artichaut et de citron confit au cari

PREPARATION: 30 minutes
COOKING: 45 minutes

For a 2¼-pound jar:

4 large artichokes
2 lemons
1 onion, finely chopped
1-inch piece of fresh ginger, grated
½ teaspoon curry powder
1 tablespoon olive oil
1 tablespoon white vinegar
Fine salt, gros sel

Squeeze one of the lemons. Cook the artichokes in a pan of water with 1 tablespoon gros sel and the lemon juice for 45 minutes. Drain (leaves down) in a sieve.

Heat the olive oil in a pan, sweat the onion gently, and add the ginger and curry powder. Cook for 15 seconds.

Cut the second lemon in half. Put it in a pan, cover with cold water, and boil for 2 minutes. Throw out the water and repeat this process twice. Cut the lemon into very small dice and add it to the spice mixture.

Take off the artichoke leaves and the hairy choke, keeping only the artichoke bottoms. Cut these into very small dice and add to the spice mixture. Cook for 5 minutes over low heat. Add the vinegar and salt. Pour into a jar, let cool, seal hermetically. Keep in the refrigerator.

To use: This strong-flavored salsa goes well with lamb, duck, or fish poached in white wine.

Green asparagus salsa

Asperges vertes aux épices façon "cornichon"

PREPARATION: 25 minutes
MARINATION: 1 month

For a 2-cup (50 cl) jar:

8 ounces (250 g) thin green asparagus
1 tablespoon coriander seeds
1 tablespoon whole Szechuan pepper
1½ cups (40 cl) rice vinegar
1 tablespoon sugar
½ teaspoon gros sel

Wash the asparagus and dry carefully. Cut the points about 1½ inches (4 cm) from the top and the stems in ¾-inch (2 cm) slices. Throw away the bottom 2 inches (5 cm), which are too tough. Put the spices in a jar, then add the asparagus.

Boil the vinegar with the salt and sugar. Pour it boiling into the jar. Close the jar immediately. Let marinate for a month before using.

To use: This unusual, delicious salsa, rather like a pickle, goes well with cold meats. You can vary the spices according to your taste.

Asparagus stems break easily at the point where they become unedible. The tough bits can be used in a stock for soups and sauces.—**TRANS.**

11 Desserts

Curried figs with green apples
Cari de figues aux pommes vertes

SERVES 4 | PREPARATION: 20 minutes
COOKING: 8 minutes

16 plump figs
4 Granny Smith apples
Juice of ½ lemon
¼ teaspoon fennel seeds
½ teaspoon curry powder
½ cup (4 oz, 100 g) sugar
6 tablespoons (4 oz, 100 g) thick crème fraîche

Carefully peel the figs with the point of a knife. Do not peel the apples, but cut each into 6 pieces. Core them, then blend them with the lemon juice. Put the sugar and 2 tablespoons water in a large pan (large enough to hold the figs later, without piling them up). Mix and cook gently to get a blond caramel.

Press the apple pulp through a sieve, pushing hard to get the most juice, over the caramel on the heat. Add the fennel seeds and curry powder. When this mixture boils, arrange the figs on the bottom of the pan. Cover and cook for 7 to 8 minutes. Let them cool in their juice.

To serve, put the figs in 4 shallow dishes. Mix the juice with the crème fraîche. Coat the figs with the sauce.

CHEF'S COMMENTS: This dish can be served warm or cold. The fig, which is both a fruit and a vegetable, goes very well with curry.

Blancmange with coconut and long pepper
Blanc-manger à la noix de coco et au poivre long

SERVES 6	PREPARATION: 20 minutes COOKING: 10 minutes REFRIGERATION: 2 to 3 hours

- 2 cups (50 cl) milk
- 2 cups (50 cl) whipping (heavy) cream
- ⅝ cup (5 oz, 125 g) sugar
- 1½ cups (6 oz, 150 g) grated coconut
- ¼ teaspoon long pepper (milled in a pepper mill), or substitute nutmeg
- 1 envelope gelatin, equivalent to 7 g, or 5 sheets)
- A little brown sugar (optional)

Heat the milk with the coconut. Leave it off the heat for 10 minutes to absorb the milk. Whip the cream with the sugar until firm. Keep in the refrigerator. Soak the gelatin in water.

Blend the milk and coconut for 1 minute, then press the mixture through a sieve to extract all the coconut milk. Add the gelatin to the warm milk and mix well to dissolve. Let cool. Using a plastic spatula, gently add the whipped cream and the long pepper to the milk.

Divide the mixture into individual dishes. Refrigerate for 2 to 3 hours. Serve as is, sprinkled with brown sugar, browned under the broiler (for this be sure your dishes are heat resistant), or sprinkled with a bit of grated coconut. →

CHEF'S COMMENTS: Here is an exotic version of our traditional almond blancmange. The spicy, vanilla flavor of long pepper is marvelous with sweet dishes.

Long ago this dish might have had almonds, rose water, orange flower water, and other Middle Eastern flavors. We have at times made coconut milk, but we also have used packaged or canned coconut milk. Make certain you get the unsweetened variety. Also note that pepper often goes well with sweets.—**TRANS.**

Spiced Queen of Sheba cake
Reine de Saba aux épices

SERVES 6 to 8

PREPARATION: 30 minutes
COOKING: 30 minutes
REFRIGERATION: 2 hours

- 8 ounces (200 g) dark chocolate, broken into pieces
- ⅔ cup (2 oz, 50 g) powdered cocoa
- 4 eggs
- ¼ teaspoon powdered cinnamon
- ½ teaspoon powdered coriander
- 1 teaspoon white sesame seeds
- 2 cloves
- 1 cup (4 oz, 100 g) chopped almonds
- 1 cup (4 oz, 100 g) chopped walnuts
- 1 cup (4 oz, 100 g) chopped hazelnuts
- 1 cup (6 oz, 150 g) chopped dried apricots
- ¾ cup (6 oz, 150 g) sugar
- ½ cup (4 oz, 100 g) butter + a little for the cake mold
- 1½ cups (6 oz, 150 g) flour + 6 tablespoons for the cake mold
- ½ tablespoon baking powder
- 6 tablespoons (10 cl) whipping (heavy) cream
- 6 tablespoons (10 cl) milk

Preheat the oven to 325°F (160°C).

Boil 6½ tablespoons (100 g) sugar and the cloves in ¾ cup (20 cl) water for 1 minute. Set the syrup aside. In a bowl, combine the nuts and apricots. In another bowl, mix the flour, baking powder, and cocoa. Melt the butter and set aside. →

Break the eggs into a bowl and whisk for a few seconds. Add the rest of the sugar (5½ tablespoons) and beat to get a firm mixture. Add the nuts and apricots, the flour-cocoa mixture, the melted butter, and the spices. Mix carefully with a spatula.

Butter and flour a mold 10 inches in diameter. Pour in the mixture and bake for 30 minutes in the oven.

Remove from the oven and pour on the syrup, without unmolding. Let cool, then unmold onto a board.

Bring the cream and milk to a boil, remove from heat, then add the chocolate. Whisk well. Let it cool, then refrigerate. When the chocolate has thickened, coat the cake and refrigerate for 2 hours.

It is best to take the cake out 1 hour before serving.

CHEF'S COMMENTS: Dark chocolate goes very well with spices. You can try other combinations. You will be surprised by the results.

Apple fondant with ginger
Fondant de pommes au gingembre

SERVES 6	PREPARATION: 25 minutes COOKING: 45 minutes REFRIGERATION: 12 hours

6½ pounds (3 kg) apples (Cox Orange, rennets)
6-inch piece (4 oz, 100 g) fresh ginger, or ¾ cup (3½ oz, 70 g) candied ginger
5 eggs
¾ cup (6 oz, 150 g) butter, cut in small pieces
¾ cup (6 oz, 150 g) sugar
1½ envelopes gelatin (equivalent to 10 g, or 8 sheets)

Soak the gelatin in cold water. Peel and core the apples, and cut into fine slices. In a large pan, stew the apples with the sugar, mixing into a puree with a whisk. Grate the fresh ginger (or chop finely the candied ginger) and add to the apples.

Preheat the oven to 350°F (180°C).

Off the heat, whisk into the apple puree the butter, the eggs one by one, then the gelatin. Whisk to get a smooth mixture (you can use a handheld mixer or a stick blender). Line a mold 12 inches (30 cm) in diameter and 2 inches (5 cm) tall with aluminum foil or parchment paper. Pour in the apple mixture, which should not be more than 1¼ (3 cm) inches high—taller than that and you might have problems serving it. Cook in a bain-marie in the oven for 45 minutes. Let it cool and refrigerate overnight.

Unmold the cake by turning it over on a plate, removing the paper. You can serve the cake with a caramel sauce or a crème anglaise.*

→

CHEF'S COMMENTS: This dessert will melt in your mouth. The apple and ginger complement each other.

We have a store-bought bottle of caramelized sugar that often comes in handy.

*Crème anglaise (English cream) is a basic sauce for many desserts in French cooking. It is made from 7 tablespoons (3½ oz, 90 g) sugar, 3 egg yolks, a pinch of cornstarch, and 1 cup (25 cl) of milk, plus vanilla or another flavoring. Beat the egg yolks with the sugar, add the cornstarch, and dilute with the boiling milk and the vanilla. Put over low heat, stirring constantly, and remove the moment it approaches the first boil.—**TRANS.**

Raspberry soup with smoked tea and nutmeg
Soupe de framboises au thé fumé et à la noix de muscade

SERVES 4

PREPARATION: 20 minutes
COOKING: 5 minutes

- 1 pound (400 g) raspberries
- 3 tablespoons smoked tea leaves
- 1 pinch of grated nutmeg
- 8 egg yolks
- 2 cups (50 cl) milk
- ¾ cup (20 cl) whipping (heavy) cream
- 1 cup (8 oz, 200 g) sugar

In a bowl, whisk the egg yolks and sugar until they become light and fluffy.

Put the tea in a pan, cover with 4 tablespoons water, and bring to a boil. Add the milk and bring back to a boil. Remove from the heat and cover the pan. Let infuse for 10 minutes.

Whisk the cream until it is firm, add the nutmeg, and refrigerate.

Bring the milk back to a boil and pour through a sieve over the egg yolks, whisking well. Put this mixture in a pan and heat gently for 10 seconds, stirring with a wooden spoon, just until the mixture coats the spoon. Pour into a bowl and beat for 1 minute. Refrigerate.

When the egg-milk mixture is cold, mix it gently with →

the whipped cream. Put the raspberries in soup bowls and coat them with the cream.

CHEF'S COMMENTS: Chinese smoked teas are marvelous in this type of dessert. They give the sauce a refreshing aroma. For me these teas are a spice.

Yes, cooking with smoked tea is a discovery.—**TRANS.**

Crème brûlée with caraway seeds

Crème brûlée au carvi

SERVES about 10	PREPARATION: 20 minutes COOKING: 40 minutes REFRIGERATION: 1 hour 30 minutes

8 egg yolks
2¾ cups (70 cl) heavy cream
1½ cups (40 cl) milk
2 tablespoons caraway seeds
¾ cup (6 oz, 150 g) sugar
¼ cup (2 oz, 50 g) brown sugar

Infuse 1 cup (30 cl) milk with the caraway seeds over low heat, keeping the temperature close to boiling for 20 minutes.

Mix the egg yolks and sugar until the mixture turns light, add the cream, and mix well. Refrigerate for 30 minutes.

Heat the oven to 200°F (100°C).

Blend the cooked milk and caraway with a little fresh milk to get 1 cup (30 cl) of liquid. Sieve this and remove the caraway seeds, setting them aside. Mix 1 tablespoon of seeds with the cream and egg yolk mixture, then add the milk, whisking to blend.

Pour this mixture in 10 crème brûlée molds (ovenproof dishes about 4 inches in diameter and 1½ inches high). Sprinkle the rest of the caraway seeds on the molds and bake for 30 to 40 minutes in a bain-marie in the oven. The cream should not be liquid, but have a trembling texture. If your oven is not large, bake these in two batches. Refrigerate for 1 hour. →

Sprinkle the molds with brown sugar and caramelize them with a kitchen torch or under the grill (in which case you must watch the caramelization carefully).

CHEF'S COMMENTS: Caraway is seldom used but is very appealing. Use freshly bought seeds to get the maximum flavor.

We had old, dried caraway seeds that were useless. The fresh ones get sprinkled on fish, chicken, salads, cheese.—**TRANS.**

Poached pears with spicy tapioca
Poires pochées au tapioca d'épices

SERVES 4 | PREPARATION: 20 minutes
COOKING: 50 minutes

4 pears (Comice or another good variety)
1 orange (with untreated skin), cut into ½-inch (1 cm) rounds
1 clove
6 coriander seeds
6 peppercorns
1 stick cinnamon
2 tablespoons tapioca
4 cups (1 liter) red wine
1 cup (8 oz, 200 g) sugar
1 tablespoon whipping (heavy) cream
A little milk (optional)

Peel and core the pears without removing the stem. Put side by side in a pan. Add the spices, the red wine, the sugar, and the unpeeled orange. Cook, covered, over medium heat for about 30 minutes, depending on the firmness of the pears. Check with the point of a knife; it should go in without much resistance.

Move the pears to a shallow dish. Filter the wine through a sieve, over the cooking pan, and heat it. When it boils, add the tapioca in a stream and whisk. Cook gently for 15 minutes, uncovered. Halfway through add ½ cup of water to thin the sauce. Stir often so the sauce doesn't stick. The tapioca is cooked when the "pearls" are completely transparent. →

Pour the cream on the tapioca mixture. If the sauce is too thick, thin it with a little milk. When it is warm, coat the pears and serve.

You can also serve this dessert cold, in which case you will probably need to thin the sauce.

CHEF'S COMMENTS: For this recipe choose the smallest pearls of tapioca you can find. Japanese tapioca is best and can be found in Asian shops. It is used often for desserts in Asia. In street shops in Malaysia you can buy a tapioca-based dessert served with coconut milk and palm sugar. Delicious! In my recipe, the spices and wine create a warm flavor.

If you cannot get untreated oranges, blanch the orange in boiling water briefly to remove the wax.—**TRANS.**

Banana cake with candied ginger
Gâteau de bananes au gingembre confit

SERVES 9

PREPARATION: 25 minutes
COOKING: 1 hour 15 minutes

- 5 bananas
- 1 cup (4 oz, 100 g) candied ginger
- 4 eggs
- 6 tablespoons (10 cl) milk
- 1¼ cups (10 oz, 250 g) softened butter + 1 tablespoon for the mold
- 1¼ cups (10 oz, 250 g) sugar
- 4 cups (1 pound, 400 g) flour + 2 tablespoons for the mold
- 2 tablespoons (⅔ oz, 20 g) baking powder

Preheat the oven to 325°F (160°C).

Chop the candied ginger in small pieces. Peel the bananas and crush them with a potato masher or puree in a food processor until smooth.

Mix the flour, baking powder, and ginger with the bananas. In another bowl beat 1¼ cups softened butter and the sugar with a whisk. Add the eggs one by one, beating after each egg. Combine the two mixtures with a whisk and gently add the milk.

Butter and flour a large cake mold and fill it ⅔ full. Cook for 1 hour 15 minutes in the oven. Let it almost totally cool before unmolding. Keep it in the refrigerator and serve it in slices ½-inch (1 cm) thick. →

CHEF'S COMMENTS: This is a recipe I brought back from Asia, where the local people loved it. The tastes of banana and ginger are almost complementary.

This is a variation on a typically American banana cake, with the addition of candied ginger. The use of candied rather than fresh ginger is interesting.—**TRANS.**

Stewed apricots with vanilla and long pepper
Compote d'abricots à la vanille et au poivre long

SERVES 4	PREPARATION: 10 minutes COOKING: 10 minutes MACERATING: 30 minutes REFRIGERATION: 12 hours

25 ripe apricots
Juice of 1 lemon
3 vanilla beans
5 Indonesian long pepper beans (or substitute one turn of a pepper mill)
½ cup (4 oz, 100 g) sugar

Cut the apricots in half and remove the stones. Put them in a pan with the sugar and lemon juice. Let them macerate for 30 minutes.

Cut the vanilla beans in half lengthwise, scrape the seeds, and mix them with the apricots. Add the long pepper cut in ½-inch (1 cm) pieces. Cook, covered, over low heat for 8 to 10 minutes, stirring gently so as not to damage the fruit.

Keep in the refrigerator. Serve the next day, when the vanilla and long pepper have added their flavors to the fruit.

CHEF'S COMMENTS: In summer, when apricots are ripe, vanilla blends its flavors with those of the fruit. This dessert should be served quite cold. The long pepper has a complex flavor. If you don't crush the bean, it is not too spicy and can be used in sweet dishes.

Chocolate cake with nutmeg and vanilla

Gâteau coulant au chocolat, muscade et vanille

SERVES 6 to 8	PREPARATION: 30 minutes COOKING: 6 minutes

- 10 ounces (250 g) dark chocolate with 70 percent cocoa
- ½ cup (2 oz, 50 g) chopped hazelnuts
- ¼ teaspoon freshly ground nutmeg
- 1 vanilla bean
- 1 egg + 2 yolks
- ½ cup (4 oz, 100 g) butter, cut into small pieces, + 1 tablespoon for the molds
- ¼ cup (2 oz, 50 g) sugar
- 3 tablespoons (¾ oz, 20 g) flour + 3 tablespoons for the molds

Preheat the oven to 350°F (180°C).

Melt the chocolate in the microwave or in a bain-marie. Whisk in the butter.

Cut the vanilla bean in two and scrape out the seeds. Add them and the grated nutmeg to the melted chocolate.

Fill a pan halfway with water and bring to a boil.

In a bowl, beat the egg, yolks, and sugar for 30 seconds. Put the bowl over the simmering water and beat for 30 seconds, then remove from the heat and beat for another 30 seconds.

Pour the flour in a stream over the chocolate, then add the hazelnuts and the egg-sugar mixture. Mix gently. Butter and flour 8 small molds. Cook in the oven for 6 minutes. Serve immediately.

CHEF'S COMMENTS: Warm, runny chocolate is one of the summits of good food. The nutmeg adds an unexpected touch.

This is a hazelnut version of a kind of chocolate cake that has become the favorite of Paris and which too often is found without much variation on menus.—**TRANS.**

Chocolate quenelles with jasmine
Quenelles de chocolat au jasmin

SERVES 5	PREPARATION: 20 minutes COOKING: 5 minutes REFRIGERATION: 6 hours

1½ pounds (600 g) dark chocolate, broken into small pieces
5 teaspoons (⅓ oz, 10 g) jasmine tea leaves
3 egg yolks
2 cups (50 cl) milk
2 cups (50 cl) crème fraîche
¼ cup (2 oz, 50 g) sugar

Mix the sugar and egg yolks in a bowl, beating until the mixture turns light and fluffy.

Bring the milk, cream, and tea leaves to a boil in a pan. Remove from heat. Cover and let infuse for 5 minutes. Heat again to boiling.

Pour the cream through a fine sieve on the egg yolks, mixing well. Press the tea leaves with a spoon to extract the maximum flavor. Mix well with a whisk. Add the chocolate and stir until the mixture is smooth. Refrigerate for 6 hours.

When the mixture is hard, dip a soupspoon in very hot water and scrape the chocolate to make a quenelle (a spindle shape). Dip the spoon in water after each quenelle. (Or use an ice-cream scoop.)

Serve this dish with a crème anglaise flavored with vanilla or tea. The consistency of the quenelles will vary according to the chocolate you use. If the result is too soft, add 2 ounces (50 g) of chocolate.

CHEF'S COMMENTS: Jasmine becomes a spice in this recipe. With chocolate, jasmine gives a sumptuous result. Milk keeps the recipe from being too rich.

See the recipe for crème anglaise under Apple fondant with ginger. Quenelles have an elongated egg shape and are traditionally made of fish, eggs, and flour. In recent decades the word has been used for desserts presented in egglike shapes rather than round balls.—**TRANS.**

Pumpkin pie with cinnamon
Tarte au potimarron et à la cannelle

SERVES 8

PREPARATION: 45 minutes
COOKING: 15 minutes
RESTING: 2 hours

- 2 pounds (800 g) peeled and seeded pumpkin
- 1 lemon
- ½ cup (2 oz, 50 g) chopped almonds
- ½ teaspoon powdered cinnamon
- 2 eggs + 1 yolk
- 1 cup crème fraîche
- ½ cup (4 oz, 100 g) butter, cut into small pieces
- 2 cups (8 oz, 225 g) flour
- ½ cup (4 oz, 100 g) brown sugar
- Salt

Put the pumpkin in the microwave for 15 minutes in a closed container (or bake in a moderate oven until tender). Drain.

In a large bowl, mix (with your fingers) the flour, egg yolk, a pinch of salt, and the butter. Grate the lemon skin and squeeze the juice, adding both to the pastry. Knead gently to form a ball, wrap it in a wet towel, and refrigerate for 2 hours.

Preheat the oven to 350°F (180°C).

Roll out the dough and fill a pie dish 10 to 12 inches (25 to 30 cm) in diameter. Refrigerate for 10 minutes. Prick the dough with a fork and bake for 15 minutes.

In a blender, puree the pumpkin, cream, the whole eggs, the brown sugar, and the cinnamon for 15 seconds. Pour into the pie shell. Sprinkle with chopped almonds, return to the oven, and bake for 45 minutes.

Serve at room temperature.

CHEF'S COMMENTS: This is a great classic in the United States, where they often use too much cinnamon.

This variation on pumpkin pie, with little cinnamon but with lemon zest and chopped almonds, will make a new Thanksgiving dessert.—**TRANS.**

Roasted pineapple with caramelized spices
Ananas rôti au caramel d'épices

SERVES 4 to 6	PREPARATION: 30 minutes COOKING: 40 minutes

- 1 ripe pineapple
- 8 long pepper beans (or, if not available add a bit more ginger)
- 1 tablespoon (½ oz, 10 g) ginger, peeled and cut into thin strips
- 1 vanilla bean
- 1¾ cups (14 oz, 350 g) sugar

Cut the base of the pineapple so it will stand up. Peel from the top to the bottom, and remove the "eyes" following a spiral pattern.

Preheat the oven to 400°F (200°C).

Heat a heavy-bottom pan, pour in half the sugar, and make a caramel, stirring with a wooden spoon. Then add the rest of the sugar and continue stirring until the sugar is completely dissolved and the caramel is smooth.

Lower the heat and add 6 tablespoons water (be careful it doesn't splatter and burn you). Mix well, and repeat this procedure three times. When the caramel is well mixed, add the long peppers and the ginger. Cook for 5 minutes over low heat. Then, off the heat, add the seeds of the vanilla bean.

Put the pineapple in a roasting pan, moisten with the caramel, and bake for 20 minutes. Turn the fruit around, moisten with the liquid caramel and bake 20 more minutes.

Serve the fruit whole, or cut it in vertical slices, coated with the caramel and spices.

CHEF'S COMMENTS: Here is a festival of flavors: the peppery ginger and long pepper, and the acidity of the pineapple.

Small pineapples roasted with caramel sauce have become a popular Parisian dessert. As they tend to be sweet, adding pepper and ginger is a good idea. So might be caraway, even fresh celery bits.—**TRANS.**

Apple pie with coriander caramel
Tarte aux pommes, caramel à la coriandre

SERVES 6	PREPARATION: 30 minutes COOKING: 30 minutes RESTING: 30 minutes

18 ounces (500 g) puff pastry
18 ounces (500 g) apples (about 3 large apples)
2 tablespoons coriander seeds
4 tablespoons (2 oz, 50 g) butter + 2 tablespoons for the mold
½ cup (4 oz, 100 g) sugar
4 tablespoons (1 oz, 30 g) flour for the mold

To make the caramel, heat a heavy-bottom pan, pour in half the sugar, and stir with a wooden spoon until it colors. Then add the rest of the sugar, stirring to combine and to get a good caramel color. Lower the heat and stir in the coriander seeds. Pour the caramel in a dish and let it cool.

When the caramel has hardened, break it into small pieces and reduce it to a fine powder in a blender.

Peel the apples, cut in half, remove the seeds, and cut into fine slices. Butter and flour a pie mold. Put the puff pastry in the mold, making a high border, so that the pastry doesn't sink when cooked. Refrigerate for 30 minutes.

Preheat the oven to 350°F (180°C).

Put the apples on the pastry in a spiral pattern. Cover the surface with the caramel. Add small bits of butter, and bake for about 30 minutes, longer if needed to get a good color. Serve warm.

CHEF'S COMMENTS: Coriander and caramel give the apples a slightly peppery taste. If you buy a prepared puff pastry, fresh or frozen, already rolled out, this recipe is easier.

Phyllo dough is a possible substitute. Note once more the contrast in textures as well as flavors.—**TRANS.**

Licorice chocolate tart

Tarte fondante au chocolat et à la réglisse

SERVES 8 to 10	PREPARATION: 15 minutes COOKING: 30 minutes RESTING: 2 hours

- 12 ounces (350 g) dark chocolate, broken into pieces
- ½ teaspoon powdered licorice
- 9 egg yolks
- 3⅞ cups (95 cl) whipping (heavy) cream
- 1 cup (25 cl) milk
- ¾ cup (6 oz, 150 g) sugar
- 1 tablespoon icing sugar
- 1 stick of licorice

Bring the milk to a boil and whisk in the chocolate, then remove from heat. In a large bowl, add the sugar to the egg yolks and beat until you get a frothy cream. Add 2⅞ cups (70 cl) of whipping cream and combine well. Then mix in the chocolate.

Preheat the oven to 325°F (160°C).

Put parchment paper or aluminum foil in a mold 12 inches (30 cm) in diameter and 2 inches (5 cm) high. Add the chocolate mixture and bake for 30 minutes. When the tart is cooked, let it cool, then refrigerate for 2 hours or until firm.

Unmold the tart by pulling on the ends of the paper. If it sticks, heat the bottom of the mold over a flame, then unmold. Whip the remaining cream (1 cup, 25 cl) with the icing sugar and the powdered licorice to get firm peaks. Slice the tart and top each piece with a tablespoon of whipped cream.

Cut the licorice stick in two, then slit lengthwise to get matchstick pieces. Use these to decorate the whipped cream.

CHEF'S COMMENTS: Here is a dessert that will make you think of your childhood, when you used to chew licorice on the way to school. Licorice is a typical French spice.

We had never heard of powdered licorice, but it can be obtained from specialty stores. Try Google.—**TRANS.**

Roasted mango with black sesame seeds and flat parsley

Mangue rôtie au sésame noir et au persil plat

SERVES 4	PREPARATION: 25 minutes COOKING: 10 minutes

- 2 ripe but firm mangoes
- 1 bunch flat parsley
- 1 tablespoon black sesame seeds
- 6 tablespoons (10 cl) whipping (heavy) cream
- 3 tablespoons acacia honey
- ½ cup (4 oz, 100 g) sugar
- ½ teaspoon toasted sesame oil
- 1 teaspoon icing sugar

Boil the sugar in 3 tablespoons (5 cl) water to get a syrup. Set aside.

Wash the parsley leaves. Cut the mangoes in two and remove the stone. (The stone is toward the flat side of the mango.) Remove the flesh from each half of the mango with a soup spoon and cut into 1-inch (2 cm) pieces.

Heat the honey in a frying pan. When it caramelizes lightly, add the mangoes. Cook for 5 minutes over low heat, stirring often. Put the mangoes in four bowls. Drain the parsley leaves and puree in a blender with the syrup for 30 seconds. Set aside.

Beat the cream with the icing sugar. When it is firm, add the sesame oil. Pour the parsley sauce over the mangoes. Lightly heat a spoon and make quenelles (spindle shapes) with the whipped cream. Serve the mangoes with whipped cream on the side. Sprinkle with the sesame seeds and serve immediately.

CHEF'S COMMENTS: Toasted sesame goes very well with the taste of mangoes.

Not everyone loves Delacourcelle's use of parsley with fruit. If you don't, use a different herb or celery.—**TRANS.**

Fruit and garam masala crumble

Crumble “Catherine” aux fruits et au garam masala

SERVES 4	PREPARATION: 40 minutes COOKING: 1 hour MACERATING: 1 hour

2 apples (rennets)
14 ounces (400 g) strawberries
18 ounces (500 g) rhubarb stalks
1 tablespoon garam masala
1 cup (4 oz, 100 g) flour
½ cup (4 oz, 100 g) butter
½ cup (4 oz, 100 g) sugar
½ cup (2 oz, 50 g) chopped almonds
¼ cup (2 oz, 50 g) brown sugar

Peel and wash the rhubarb and cut into pieces 1 inch (2 cm) long. Put them on a plate and dust with half the brown sugar. Let them macerate for 1 hour.

Preheat the oven to 350°F (180°C).

Stem and wash the strawberries and cut them in half. Peel and core the apples and cut into ½-inch (1 cm) dice.

Drain the rhubarb in a sieve. In a bowl, mix the strawberries, apples, and rhubarb with the rest of the brown sugar.

Mix the flour, sugar, almonds and garam masala. Add the butter and work this mixture with your fingers to get a sandy pastry, not too homogenized (there should be a few lumps).

Put the fruit in a gratin dish, cover with the crumble pastry, and bake for 1 hour. Let cool to room temperature and serve.

CHEF'S COMMENTS: In its region of origin, northern India, garam masala is not used with sweet dishes. Its flavors go wonderfully, however, with cooked fruits.

Crumbles are wildly popular in Paris, and this recipe gives them a new twist.—**TRANS.**

Dark chocolate mousse with star anise
Mousse au chocolat noir et à l'anis étoilé

SERVES 4

PREPARATION: 35 minutes
COOKING: 5 minutes
INFUSION: 30 minutes
REFRIGERATION: 2 hours

- 7 ounces (200 g) dark chocolate
- 4 star anise, crumbled
- 4 eggs
- 2 tablespoons (4 cl) milk
- 2 tablespoons (4 cl) whipping (heavy) cream
- 2 tablespoons (1 oz, 20 g) butter
- 2 tablespoons (1 oz, 20 g) sugar

Bring the milk to a boil with the cream and the star anise. Remove from heat. Let it infuse for 30 minutes.

Cut the chocolate in pieces and melt it in a bain-marie or in a microwave. Whisk in the butter.

Separate the egg yolks from the whites. Beat the yolks lightly and add them to the warm melted chocolate. Bring the anise infusion to a boil and pour it over the chocolate through a sieve. Whisk to mix well.

Beat the egg whites to firm peaks with the sugar. Fold them gently into the chocolate mixture. Refrigerate for 2 hours. Remove ½ hour before serving.

CHEF'S COMMENTS: It is often hard to find a good flavor to go with chocolate, but star anise is one.

This is rich; serve small portions. At the restaurant it is served in tiny dishes with coffee, instead of cookies or chocolates.—**TRANS.**

Cherry and lemongrass tart
Clafoutis aux cerises et à la citronnelle

SERVES 4

PREPARATION: 20 minutes
COOKING: 25 minutes

- 1½ pounds (600 g) cherries
- 1 stalk lemongrass
- 2 eggs
- 1 cup (9 oz, 250 g) whipping (heavy) cream
- 2 tablespoons (1 oz, 20 g) butter
- 5 tablespoons (1 oz, 25 g) flour
- 5 tablespoons (2 oz, 60 g) brown sugar

Preheat the oven to 350°F (180°C).

Stem the cherries, wash, and drain. Chop the lemongrass, put it in a saucepan with the cream, and bring to a boil. Let it infuse for 10 minutes off the heat, and let it cool.

Mix the brown sugar, eggs, and flour to get a smooth batter. Pour the cream through a sieve over this mixture and beat until smooth.

Butter a pie dish, a quiche dish, or any ovenproof pan large enough that mixture is no more than ½ inch (1 cm) high. Pour the mixture into this dish, add the cherries (do not remove the stones), and bake for 25 minutes. Let it cool for 20 minutes. Serve, advising your guests to watch out for the stones.

CHEF'S COMMENTS: Lemongrass adds an original touch to this classic recipe.

The French love clafoutis; some others consider it deadly rich. Although they can be made with any fruit, this one is worthy of love.—**TRANS.**

Apples roasted with garam masala
Pommes rôties au garam masala

SERVES 4

PREPARATION: 40 minutes
COOKING: 20 minutes

- 2 Granny Smith apples
- ½ cup (2 oz, 50 g) chopped walnuts
- 6 tablespoons (2 oz, 50 g) raisins
- ½ cup (2 oz, 50 g) chopped almonds
- ¾ cup (4 oz, 100 g) pitted dates
- 4 pinches garam masala
- ½ teaspoon mustard seeds
- 1 tablespoon (½ oz, 20 g) butter
- 2 tablespoons thick crème fraîche
- 1 tablespoon brown sugar

Boil the mustard seeds in 2 cups (50 cl) water for 5 minutes. Drain. Mix the nuts and raisins, cover with water, and boil for 5 minutes to plump them. Drain.

Preheat the oven to 350°F (180°C).

Cut the apples in two without peeling. Remove the core. Place them, hollow side up, in a ovenproof dish. Add to each a small nut of butter, a little brown sugar, chopped almonds, and a pinch of garam masala. Bake for 20 minutes.

Puree the dates and crème fraîche in a blender. Add the walnuts, raisins, and mustard seed.

Remove the apples from the oven, let cool to room temperature.

With two spoons, make a spindle shape from the cream and add it to each apple.

CHEF'S COMMENTS: Garam masala, an Indian combination of spices, is normally used for savory dishes. Using a small amount with sugar gives a delicious, surprising taste.

While garam masala can now be found in most supermarket spice racks, as well as Indian shops, it can be made by grinding together black pepper, black cumin, cinnamon, cloves, cardamom seeds, and coriander seeds. There are many variations. See also the recipe under garam masala in the Description of Spices. Delacourcelle likes to mix garam masala with apples and other fruits.—**TRANS.**

Two-sesame chocolate cream
Crème chocolat aux deux sésames

SERVES 4 to 6	PREPARATION: 30 minutes COOKING: 40 minutes

6 ounces (150 g) dark chocolate, broken into small pieces
1 tablespoon blond sesame seeds
1 tablespoon black sesame seeds
1 egg
9 tablespoons (15 cl) whipping (heavy) cream
¾ cup (20 cl) milk
4 tablespoons toasted sesame oil

Preheat the oven to 200°F (100°C).

Bring the milk and cream to a boil and pour over the chocolate, mixing well with a whisk. Remove from heat, add the egg, continuing to whisk, then the toasted sesame oil. Whisk again.

Fill 4 or 6 small molds or 1 large mold, 1 inch high. Cook in a bain-marie in the oven for 40 minutes.

Remove the molds from the oven and let them cool. Mix the two varieties of seeds and sprinkle over the creams. Serve at room temperature.

You can cook these the day before and remove them from the refrigerator 3 hours before serving. In this case, sprinkle them with sesame seeds at the last moment.

CHEF'S COMMENTS: Although the Chinese don't usually like chocolate, here I am combining a typically Chinese flavor, toasted sesame oil, with dark, bitter chocolate. Two territories meet and blend together happily.

Look for toasted sesame oil in an oriental shop. It has an excellent flavor, quite different from other sesame oil. This dessert is not at all sweet, and probably won't appeal to children. Note: no butter and only one egg. A beautiful dish to look at as well as eat.—**TRANS.**

Caramel jam with salt and pepper
Confiture de lait au poivre et au sel

PREPARATION: 10 minutes
COOKING: about 1 hour

For 2 jars:

1 quart (1 liter) milk
2¼ cups (18 oz, 500 g) sugar
7 tablespoons (100 g) acacia honey
Pinch of sel de Guérande
2 pinches of white pepper, coarsely ground

In a large pan, bring the milk to a boil with the sugar and honey and cook gently for 1 hour to get a caramel color.

Pour the mixture into a bowl, add the salt and pepper, and beat until smooth. Let cool in the refrigerator. Serve on grilled bread or brioche.

CHEF'S COMMENTS: The salt and pepper mixed with the caramel flavor whets the appetite. I created this dish for the birthday of a friend with "salt and pepper" hair. He loved it. Be careful, since the milk overflows easily during cooking. My mother used a thick round of glass in the pan to keep the milk from overflowing. You can still find such gadgets in specialty stores. A glass cover of a jam jar can make a good substitute.

A variation on the cooked milk dessert found around the world. We keep the heat very low, but then it can take twice as long.—**TRANS.**

Pear, lime peel, and sumac jam

Confiture de poires et d'écorce de citron vert au sumac

PREPARATION: 20 minutes
COOKING: 30 minutes

For 2 jars:

1 lime
2¼ pounds (1 kg) pears
1 tablespoon powdered sumac
3 cups (21 oz, 600 g) sugar

Peel the lime with a vegetable peeler. Squeeze the lime and save the juice. Put the peel in a pan, cover with 1 quart (1 liter) of water, bring to a boil, and cook for 2 minutes. Throw out the water. Repeat this procedure twice. Process the peel in a blender to make a puree.

Peel and seed the pears, and cut them in small pieces. Moisten with the lime juice and add the sumac. Mix well.

In a heavy-bottom pan, combine all the ingredients and cook for 30 minutes over low heat, stirring often. Pour this mixture directly into jam jars, close them, and turn them over. Let them cool upside down. When they are lukewarm, turn them back over. Keep in the refrigerator.

CHEF'S COMMENTS: The acidic and fruity flavor of the sumac added to the pears gives this jam a special character.

An interesting combination of flavors worth experimenting with.—**TRANS.**

Strawberry jam with star anise
Confiture de fraises à l'anis étoilé

PREPARATION: 25 minutes
COOKING: 45 minutes
MACERATING: 30 minutes

For 2 jars:

- 2¼ pounds (1 kg) strawberries
- Juice of 1 lemon
- 5 star anise
- 1 pinch of white pepper
- 3¼ cups (25 oz, 700 g) sugar

Stem and wash the strawberries, and cut them in half. Moisten them with lemon juice and sprinkle with 4 tablespoons of sugar. Let them macerate for 30 minutes, then drain.

In a heavy-bottom pan combine the strawberries, the rest of the sugar, the star anise, and the white pepper. Cook for 45 minutes over low heat, taking care that the strawberries don't stick.

Pour into jam jars. Close the jars and turn them upside down. When the jam is cool, turn the jars over. Keep in the refrigerator.

CHEF'S COMMENTS: The star anise needs several days to give off its flavor, so you must be patient to taste this jam under the best conditions.

“My mother’s” cake with walnuts, vanilla, and cinnamon

Gâteau de ma mère aux noix, à la vanille et à la cannelle

SERVES 6 to 8 | PREPARATION: 30 minutes
COOKING: 35 minutes

5 eggs
⅝ cup (5 oz, 125 g) butter, softened
1½ cups (6 oz, 150 g) walnut halves
1 cup (4 oz, 100 g) ground almonds
½ teaspoon ground cinnamon
1 vanilla bean
1½ cups (12 oz, 300 g) sugar
1 cup (4 oz, 100 g) flour

Preheat the oven to 400°F (200°C). Butter a cake mold and line it with aluminum foil.

Chop the walnuts in the blender and mix with the ground almonds.

Beat the butter with the sugar for 2 minutes, using an electric beater, to get a light, creamy consistency. Add the eggs one by one, continuing to beat. Add the flour, the nuts, and the cinnamon.

Cut the vanilla bean in half lengthwise with a small knife and scrape out the seeds. Add the seeds to the batter. Pour into the mold and bake for 35 minutes. Let it cool before →

unmolding. If you want to keep the cake moist, wrap it in plastic wrap while warm.

CHEF'S COMMENTS: My mother often makes this marvelous cake for her grandchildren during vacation; with the vanilla and cinnamon, you will eat more than you should.

We wish we had such a mother.—**TRANS.**

Cinnamon cookies
Sablés à la cannelle

SERVES 6	PREPARATION: 30 minutes COOKING: 12 minutes REFRIGERATION: 30 minutes

- 1¼ cups (10 oz, 250 g) butter, cut into small pieces, + 2 tablespoons for the cookie sheet
- ½ cup (4 oz, 100 g) sugar
- 3½ cups (14 oz, 350 g) flour + 4 tablespoons for the cookie sheet
- ½ teaspoon ground cinnamon
- 1 cup (8 oz, 200 g) crystallized sugar

In a large bowl, combine the butter, sugar, flour, and cinnamon. Mix with the tips of your fingers, lightly, breaking up the dough to get a consistency like sand. Take part of the dough, squash it on the table with the palm of your hand. Make a ball, then roll to 1 inch (2 cm) in diameter. Roll this in the crystallized sugar, divided for easier handling. When all the rolls are ready, refrigerate them for 30 minutes.

Preheat the oven to 350°F (180°C).

Cut the rolls into rounds ½ inch (1 cm) thick. Put the cookies on a buttered and floured baking sheet and bake for 10 to 12 minutes (depending on how done you like the cookies).

Let them cool on the sheet. Remove carefully with a metal spatula, and when they are completely cold, keep in a hermetically sealed box. →

CHEF'S COMMENTS: These little cookies are good with coffee or for a snack. Try different spices if you have no cinnamon, but be careful not to use too much spice.

Other flavors might be lemon peel, orange peel, and chocolate. We especially like anise seeds. Caraway seeds are also possible.—**TRANS.**

Cold soufflé with ricotta and poppy seeds

Soufflé froid au fromage blanc et aux graines de pavot

SERVES 6	PREPARATION: 20 minutes COOKING: 3 minutes REFRIGERATION: 3 to 4 hours

- 6 eggs
- 11 ounces (300 g) ricotta (or fromage blanc, if available)
- 6 tablespoons (10 cl) whipping (heavy) cream
- 1 tablespoon poppy seeds
- ½ teaspoon cornstarch
- ¾ cup (6 oz, 150 g) sugar
- ¼ cup Suze
- 1½ envelopes of gelatin (equivalent to 10 g, or 7 sheets)

Separate the whites from the yolks. In a pan, mix the yolks, cream, ricotta, Suze, cornstarch, and poppy seeds. Whisk over low heat until the mixture boils. Remove immediately from the heat.

Soak the gelatin in cold water. Then add to the egg yolk mixture.

Prepare a mold 10 inches (25 cm) in diameter and 1½ to 2 inches (4 to 5 cm) tall. Beat the egg whites gently with a pinch of sugar until they are very creamy, then add the rest of the sugar, beating more vigorously, to get firm peaks (this will prevent the egg whites from becoming grainy).

Pour the egg yolk–ricotta mixture over the egg whites, mixing gently with a wooden spatula. Pour into the mold and refrigerate for 3 to 4 hours. →

You can serve this dessert in or out of the mold. To unmold, run the mold rapidly under hot water and turn it over very carefully.

CHEF'S COMMENTS: This is a good summer dessert—fresh, easy, and quick to prepare. The poppy seeds are crunchy.

Suze is an aperitif wine made from wild gentian flowers. It is 16 percent alcohol and rather bitter. It is delicious, and worth looking for. (Besides this recipe, it is good to drink with orange juice, as a summer aperitif.) Two other well-known brands of gentian wine are Salers and Aveze. You may need to ask your wine merchant to order it. Green chartreuse or a dry sherry might be a substitute. Avoid a too-sweet flavor. Again, notice the use of texture with the poppy seeds as well as an unusual flavor.—**TRANS.**

Description of Spices

African Pepper: Maniguette (or Seeds of Paradise)

This purely African spice comes from the coast of West Africa, especially from a region once called the "pepper coast" (present-day Liberia and Sierra Leone). It is also called Guinean pepper or malaguette. The plant (*Amomum melegueta*) comes from a rhizome. The seeds grow in large pods.

For a long time Maniguette competed with black pepper, which was much more expensive. It substituted for pepper before the pepper route was fully established. From the sixteenth century, when pepper was readily available, Maniguette was used to flavor beer. West Africans used it in place of black pepper, which was destined for trade. Today Maniguette still comes from Africa, especially Ghana. Africans use it not only as a spice but also as a home remedy for chills. North African cuisine, especially Tunisian, uses a lot of Maniguette.

Grind this spice just before using, for its aromas are fleeting. It has a spicy and lightly lemony taste. Ground on a salad or on a steamed fish, Maniguette reveals all its flavorful character.

My favorite recipes: Tuna pâté with dill and four peppers; Duckling in honey and African pepper.

Allspice: Poivre de la Jamaïque

This is neither a pepper nor a chili pepper, but its Latin name is *Pimenta officinalis*, and its popular name in the West Indies, where it is widely used, is *pimienta*. In France it is known as four-spices, allspice, and *poivre de la Jamaïque*. In the French Caribbean it is called *bois d'Inde* (Indian wood).

The bush, of the Myrtaceae family, produces small, round berries, which are picked before they are ripe and are then dried. Their odor is strong and complex, recalling cinnamon, clove, nutmeg, and pepper (hence "four-spices"). They are used in the cuisine of Jamaica and all the Caribbean islands for marinades, cocktails, stews, and drinks. This is the spice par excellence of the islands. In France allspice is used primarily in marinades and preserved meats. Allspice deserves a better reputation than that of a spice recalling several others without a taste of its own. It can be used for its own virtues, in a pepper mill.

My favorite recipe: Tuna pâté with dill and four peppers.

Caraway Seeds: Carvi

The scientific name is *Carum carvi*, but the origin is undoubtedly the Arabic *karw'iya*. Caraway is a member of the parsley family, Umbelliferae. Cultivated primarily in northern Europe and the East, it grows wild in the Alps. The plant is harvested in summer. The stalks are thrashed like wheat, then the seeds are dried. Caraway, slightly bitter and acidic at the same time, has a less anise flavor than cumin, with which it is often confused, as they look rather alike.

Caraway has been used for five thousand years without losing its popularity. Originally a medicinal plant, it became one of the most widely used culinary spices in Europe.

It is used in many breads. In Alsace it is combined with Muenster cheese; in Hungary, with goulash, pickles, and beets; in Germany, with breads and sausages; in Morocco, with some tajines; and in Tunisia it is used in a mixture of spices called *tabel*.

My favorite recipes: Romaine lettuce and smoked salmon with caraway seeds; Spiced crusted bream; Crème brûlée with caraway seeds.

Cardamom: Cardamome

In Arabic it is *hahmama*; in Greek, *kardamon*. Latin combines these two terms under the botanical name *Amomum cardamomum*. It comes from India, in the Kardamon mountains. The plant is of the Zingiberaceae family. Like ginger and turmeric, it has rhizomes.

During the great days of Rome, cardamom was in commercial competition with pepper. It was especially used medicinally for stomach problems. It has remained a sought-after spice and still brings a high price.

The best cardamom is green. White cardamom has white beans. Black cardamom is considered a false cardamom, as its taste is different from that of the other varieties. In cooking, cardamom has a taste of camphor. It is used in many curries. In India and Afghanistan, rice is often cooked with several split cardamom beans. Cardamom is used in most Indian desserts and in coffee in several Arab countries. You must split the beans to get the seeds, which you crush with a knife blade to bring out the flavor.

My favorite recipe: Veal in a white sauce with star anise and spices.

Chewing cardamom seeds is sometimes useful to those trying to stop smoking.—**TRANS.**

Cinnamon and Chinese Cinnamon: Cannelle et Casse

The name "cinnamon" covers a fairly wide range of spices, related to the bay leaf. These barks of shrubs with a warm, penetrating odor are harvested in India, Sri Lanka, Indonesia, China, and Vietnam. The best-known variety in Europe is Ceylanese cinnamon (*Cinnamomum zeylanicum*), which comes in long, crumbly sticks, light in color and with a soft, sweet flavor. Indonesian cinnamon comes in thicker sticks and is more aromatic. Chinese cinnamon (*Cinnamomum cassia*) looks similar but has a more robust flavor; it is very flavorful and slightly bitter. In China it is used to flavor stocks and dishes cooked for a long time. This is the type of cinnamon known the longest in the West.

Cinnamon and Chinese cinnamon are used in all sorts of Asian dishes, both sweet and savory, and are used to flavor tea. In Western Europe they are mostly used for desserts and pastries, whereas in the eastern Mediterranean (Greece, Turkey, Iran) they are used for meats, especially when simmered with tomatoes. Their culinary range should be broader. They can bring a deep aroma to fish and meat.

My favorite recipes: Gray mullet roasted with orange and cinnamon; "My mother's" cake with walnuts, vanilla, and cinnamon.

Cloves: Clou de Girofle

The botanical name of the plant is *Eugenia caryophyllata*, from the Greek *karyophyllon*. In Arabic it is called *qarunfel*. In French it was first called *giroufle*, before the present *girofle* was adopted.

It comes from the tropical myrtle tree (*giroflier* in French), which originates in the Moluques, an archipelago in eastern Indonesia; it can grow to a height of fifty feet and live for 150 years. The most flavorful part of the flower is harvested by hand just before the corolla opens, as afterward a lot of flavor is lost. After drying for three days, the buds take on a red-brown color and resemble nails.

This spice was a luxury product when it arrived in Europe, and was especially prized for its medicinal qualities. Pierre Poivre broke the Dutch monopoly on trade in cloves by filching several plants and cultivating them in Madagascar.

Cloves are excellent for preserving food. They are used in marinades, especially for game. They are also used in pastries, to flavor court-bouillons, and are sometimes an element in curry powders.

My favorite recipe: Spiced Queen of Sheba cake.

Pierre Poivre translates "Peter Pepper"—an appropriate name, we think, for a spice merchant! But see the entry under Pepper, where you will learn that he named that spice for himself, so Poivre becomes an eponym (one who gives his name to a place, or an invention)!—**TRANS.**

Colombo

Colombo, a West Indian variant of Indian curry powder, comes in both paste and powder form. It includes fresh hot red pepper, garlic, turmeric, coriander, ground mustard seeds, a little clove, and cinnamon, depending on the recipe.

My favorite recipe: Caribbean mussel soup with almonds.

Coriander: Coriandre

The name comes from the Greek *koris* ("bedbug"), since some people find the odor of this herb similar to that of the crushed insect.

During antiquity this umbellifer was cultivated around the borders of the Mediterranean. Both the leaves and the seeds are used in cooking. Harvested when ripe, the plants are dried and beaten to separate the seeds. These have a spicy taste, with notes of pepper and of the zest of citrus fruits. The fresh plant is very aromatic, with a light and peppery smell. It is also called Chinese parsley or Arabic parsley. The leaves are often used in Asia, North Africa, and Latin America as we use parsley.

Ground, the seeds are used in curry powders and masala. They are excellent in vegetable dishes and are found often in Moroccan cooking. Fresh coriander (cilantro) can be used in salads. Coriander seeds can flavor stews.

In France the use of coriander is rather limited, except for dishes "à la grecque."

My favorite recipe: Apple pie with coriander caramel.

Cumin

The botanical name is *Cuminum cyminum*. While it is widely used in India, cumin comes originally from the Nile valley. It is harvested in North Africa and in Asia Minor. As with caraway seeds, the dried plant is beaten to extract the seeds. Cumin is hot and lightly anise-flavored, a bit sharp and bitter.

Cumin seed is used in curry powders and in Moroccan cooking. Eastern countries have long used it to flavor breads and pastries. In France it is the ideal companion for Muenster cheese. It is part of many spice mixtures: Indian masala, Moroccan ras el-hanout, Asian and West Indian curries, and various African dishes.

My favorite recipes: Browned rice with cumin; Sautéed rabbit with cumin; Roast pork with cumin.

Also see the description of black cumin in the entry on garam masala.—**TRANS.**

Curry: Cari

The word comes from the Tamil *kari*, which means a way of cooking. The English took the term and transformed it to *curry*, the French to *cari*.

The earliest recipes for curry are about two thousand years old and don't differ from present-day recipes. Curry powder is a mixture of spices, varied according to the dish, but always using hot red peppers, ginger, pepper, and turmeric. To this you can add coriander seeds, cumin, fenugreek, nutmeg, cloves, cinnamon, and mustard seed.

Traditional Indian cooking never uses standard curry powders, which are an English invention. It is best to do as the Indians do and make your own just before using and cook the spices gently in a little fat to bring out the flavors.

Various Asian countries, countries in the Indian Ocean, and countries in the West Indies use spice powders; their composition varies locally, but all are derived from a curry powder base: Colombo in the West Indies; *massalé* in Réunion and Mauritius; Malaysian, Indonesian, Thai curries.

Here are the proportions for a basic curry powder, to make in a blender, a coffee mill or, best, in a mortar and pestle: 1 hot red pepper, 1 tablespoon coriander seeds, 1 tablespoon cumin seeds, 1 tablespoon turmeric, 6 white or black pepper corns, ½ tablespoon powdered ginger, and 1 clove.

My favorite recipes: Curried shrimp and sweet potatoes; Curried green lentils; Chicken curry.

Dill: Aneth

The word comes from the Greek *anethon*, which describes a plant that grows very quickly. In Latin it became *anethum*. The botanical term is *Anethum graveolens*. The Nordic root of the word, which gave the English word *dill*, is *dilla*, which means "to rock." In fact, dill has long been known for its soothing effect, especially to calm small children's digestion.

This umbellifer (having flower clusters rather like umbrellas, as in parsley, for example) grows particularly in the Northern Hemisphere, around the borders of the Mediterranean. It is harvested ripe, when it has a golden brown color. The plants are thrashed, and the seeds are dried. The seeds have a deep odor that resembles caraway, lightly anise in flavor. They are very light; once dried, more than ten thousand seeds are needed to make an ounce. This was supposedly the preferred plant of witches in the Middle Ages. The fresh tufts are often used in Greek cuisine (where they are interchangeable with young fennel in the countryside), but also in Scandinavian cuisine (as in the classic Nordic salmon marinated with dill).

The seeds are used in India, in Slavic countries, and in northern Europe, where they are appreciated in vinegar preserves and cucumbers in brine ("dill pickles"). The seeds can also be used to bread fish filets or in a court-bouillon. In the bakery they are used in certain breads.

My favorite recipes: Pumpkin au gratin with dill seeds; Tuna pâté with dill and four peppers.

Fennel: Fenouil

This fragrant umbellifer, *Foeniculum vulgare*, grows wild in all the Mediterranean basin and in many parts of France. Every part of the plant is edible. Fennel stalks are used with grilled fish; the young shoots are used as an herb in rural Greece; the cultivated fennel has a bulb much appreciated in cooking. The seeds are widely used as a spice, normally in small quantities: as an ingredient in Chinese five spices, in the cuisines of India and the Near East, in vinegar marinades in central Europe, and in Italian sausages. The seeds, like the whole plant, go well with fish, but their delicate anise flavor is also excellent with vegetables and salads.

My favorite recipe: Celeriac with fennel seed.

Fenugreek: Fenugrec

This leguminous plant (one whose fruit is a kind of bean) was much appreciated in antiquity but is still not well known. This is a shame, as these small, hard, ocher-colored seeds have a unique flavor. You can reduce their bitterness by toasting them lightly before crushing them, but the odor of fresh fenugreek is sharp and pleasant. The Latin species name, *Trigonella foenum-graecum*, means "Greek hay." Formerly it was used as forage, like alfalfa; the dried plant smells strongly like hay.

In India, fenugreek (*methi*) is an essential spice. It is used in the best curry powders, particularly in those for vegetarian cooking, as it is marvelous with vegetables. Fenugreek leaves can be eaten like spinach or as flavoring in the dough for the Indian bread *naan*. Fenugreek is part of various spice mixtures, such as the *massalé* of the Indian Ocean or the *berberi* of Ethiopia, but it is rarely used alone.

My favorite recipe: Terrine of rabbit, eggplant, and fenugreek.

Garam Masala

Literally "hot spices," this is the name of a mixture of spices very popular in northern India. It is one of the many different Indian preparations called masala. Garam masala should not be confused with *massalé*, the variety of curry found in the region of the Indian Ocean. Garam masala is made of black pepper, Kashmiri black cumin (which you can find in Indian shops—a small cumin seed with a truffle taste), coriander, bay leaf, clove, and a little cinnamon. It is used at the end of cooking, as it has lighter and more volatile flavors than those of curry. Unlike the Indian tradition, I like to use it in desserts.

If you don't find garam masala in shops, you can make your own in a coffee mill: 3 tablespoons black pepper seeds, 2 tablespoons black cumin seeds (or substitute white cumin seeds), 2 sticks Ceylanese cinnamon broken in several pieces, 1 level tablespoon cloves, 1 teaspoon mace (or substitute ½ a crushed nutmeg), 2 level tablespoons green cardamom seeds (removed from the pods), 2 tablespoons coriander, and 6 bay leaves. Grind all these to a fine powder, which you can keep in a hermetically sealed jar.

My favorite recipes: Red cabbage with apples and garam masala; Scallop of veal with garam masala; Fruit and garam masala crumble.

Ginger: Gingembre

The name comes from Sanskrit *sringavera* ("horn"). In Latin it is *Zingiber officinale*. The plant is from the Zingiberaceae family (with rhizomes).

Ginger originates in India and Malaysia and is grown in regions where there is a lot of rain and sun. As it exhausts the soil quickly, rotation of crops is necessary. It is harvested after eight months, when the stems wither. Then the "hands" of the ginger (the knotty bulbs look like hands) are taken from the earth. They are scraped and often dried for export. But the fresh rhizome has the most flavor.

In supermarkets or Asian shops you can often find young ginger, tender and rose colored, not yet covered with a brown skin. Sweeter than ripened ginger, young ginger should be eaten soon after you buy it. African ginger comes in smaller "hands" than Asian ginger and has a stronger flavor. In East Africa it is used to make a strong beer.

Ginger was the first spice introduced into Europe, in part because it can easily be preserved and shipped. Sailors used a lot of it because it calms seasickness. Apicius's recipes are witness to the wide use of ginger, and gingerbread goes back to the Middle Ages and exists all over Europe.

The rhizome can be used in many ways: fresh, preserved, grated, in juice, in powder, or in vinegar. In Asian dishes, fresh, it is often used with garlic. In powder it is used in curries and some masala. Sausages and pastries are made with powdered ginger.

My favorite recipes: Tomatoes and mozzarella in ginger oil; Steamed shrimp with ginger; Banana cake with candied ginger.

Green Aniseed: Anis vert

The small seeds of the umbellifer *Pimpinella anisum* are one of the oldest-known spices, appreciated for the slightly sugary taste and as a digestive aid. This plant comes from the Middle East. Its flavor is close to that of fennel or chervil, but especially to that of star anise, although it is not of the same family. Star anise is sometimes used in place of aniseed. In India and Indonesia aniseed and fennel seed are used interchangeably, but in the Far East star anise is preferred.

Green aniseed is used in the West in Alsatian pastries and in some Mediterranean sausages, but its widest use is in making liqueurs (pastis, ouzo, Turkish raki, Spanish anis, etc.).

My favorite recipe: Rabbit legs with green aniseed.

Juniper Berries: Baies de Genièvre

This is one of the rare spices that we have never needed to import. It is also the only spice that comes from a cone-bearing tree. The juniper (*Juniperus communis*), a small, spiny tree, grows in mountainous regions. Its beautiful dark blue seeds, which are slightly bitter and sweet, ripen in two years. They are often used in the cuisines of Germany, Flanders, and the north for flavoring sauerkraut or liqueurs. In the Germanic tradition, game birds and animals are always cooked with a few juniper berries. Crush them gently before adding to your dish.

My favorite recipe: Veal kidneys with ginger and juniper berries.

Kaffir Lime Leaves: Feuilles de Limettier (also called Lime Kaffir or Combava)

The botanical name of this plant is *Citrus hystrix*. These are the leaves of a variety of Asiatic lemon tree that grows in Thailand and Malaysia, which is called in different regions *kaffir*, *makrut*, or *combava*. You will find the fruit and leaves under one of these names in Asian shops. The shrub has thorny branches; its rather thick leaves grow in pairs, as if glued together two by two. Very fragrant, the leaves have the flavors of lemon without the acidity.

The fruit of this tree resembles a dark lime with crumpled skin and a bitter taste. Fragrant but having little juice, it is used in combination with the leaves in Thai cuisine.

To extract the delicate aroma, take fresh leaves or, better still, frozen leaves (they don't travel well). This spice is often used in infusions in bouillons or soups. It is used in curries in Southeast Asia. Its flavors go well with coconut. You can use it with lemongrass.

My favorite recipes: Chanterelle mushroom cakes with kaffir lime leaves; Roasted John Dory with kaffir lime leaves.

The kaffir lime is a rough-skinned oriental lime. The leaves and skin have a strong flavor. While it is possible to obtain dried leaves, substitutes are indicated in the recipes. The kaffir lime can be scraped for its peel.—**TRANS.**

Lemongrass: Citronnelle

This tropical plant (*Cymbopogon citratus*) grows in Asia, Africa, and Latin America and is part of the family of gramineous plants. It is about twenty-five inches tall and looks like a large chive. It is harvested two or three times a year. It can be grown in Europe if exposed to light and kept from frost. It is used fresh or dried and has a very fine lemony flavor. The bulbous base can be split or crushed to get the maximum aroma. The upper part of the stalk is more bitter and should be used sparingly, and principally in infusions. Lemongrass is a magical product that enriches dishes with a fresh, citrus flavor, without acidity, and with a delicate, lasting perfume.

Verbena, melisse, and armoise are also called "citronnelle" as their flavors are close to those of *Cymbopogon citratus.*

Lemongrass is seldom used by itself; kaffir lime leaves are often added to accentuate the citrus flavors. It can be used with green curry for fish. Fresh lemongrass can be used finely chopped, like shallot, to sprinkle on a salad.

My favorite recipes: Skate marinated with lemongrass; Scallops with lemongrass; Cod with lemongrass.

While fresh lemongrass is now available in American supermarkets, it tends to dry out rapidly. Buy it fresh and keep it in water. Once dry, it can still be used for flavor if soaked in warm water.—**TRANS.**

Licorice: Réglisse

Glycyrrhiza glabra, a bush of the Leguminosae family, is related to the locust tree and is originally from China, although now it is mainly grown in India and the eastern Mediterranean. Its roots contain a sugary sap with a flavor like that of anise and fennel, but stronger. Although licorice has always been used more for its medicinal qualities than as a spice, it has long been popular in France to flavor candies and children's drinks. We all have an image of the schoolchild chewing on a licorice stick on the way to school; licorice is a French spice par excellence. I like to make the most of its affinity for chocolate.

My favorite recipe: Licorice chocolate tart.

Long Pepper: Poivre Long

This is the real *pippali* of Indian tradition; in Vedic medicine long pepper is a kind of panacea, used in many remedies. Long pepper belongs to the same family as black pepper; the fruits are harvested early and dried in the sun. They are usually grown in Indonesia and in India. The berries have a tail, resembling the silky down on willow trees. Besides its medicinal qualities, long pepper is used whole in court-bouillons and infusions. Its aroma is delicate, resembling at the same time vanilla, pepper, and nutmeg.

Long pepper has a slightly bitter taste and is a little less spicy than black pepper, although it has the strength of black pepper. If ground, it should be used sparingly. When ground it has a distinct, rich aroma.

I often use it in sauces where it gives off its flavor after being stewed for several minutes. It is also excellent in court-bouillons with fish, and to heighten the taste of caramels.

My favorite recipes: Spiced pork belly; Roasted pineapple with caramelized spices.

Mustard Seed: Graines de Moutarde

The name comes from the Latin *Mustum ardens* ("burning must"), since for many years the ground seeds were mixed with grape must.

The seeds are harvested, when ripe, from the pods before they open. They are then dried and beaten. The yellow seeds of white mustard are larger and less strong than the black or brown seeds. They do not have a strong odor and must be crushed or heated. This procedure will change the taste and must be done with care.

My favorite recipe: Lamb kidney salad with mixed spices.

Nutmeg and Mace: Noix de Muscade et Macis

The name "nutmeg" comes from the Latin *moschatus*, which comes from the Greek *moskhos*, a word of oriental origin for musk.

Nutmeg comes from a tree originating in the Moluques in Indonesia. Now Grenada produces a lot of high-quality nutmeg.

The tree has dense foliage and is about thirty to seventy feet tall. It can bear fruit until it is a hundred years old, and each tree can give forty-five pounds of fruit each year.

On the tree the fruit resembles a large green walnut about three inches in diameter. When it is ripe the fruit is yellow and splits in two to free a shell (it is possible to make a jam from this fruit). The shell is covered with a bright red or golden yellow web. This web is the mace, which is then dried. It tastes lightly spicy and a little bitter; its odors resemble that of the grated nutmeg.

In the shell is a seed, which is the nutmeg as such. This shell is exposed to the sun for two months. When it makes a ringing sound when tapped, it is broken with a hammer to extract the nut, which is the nutmeg as we know it.

Trade in nutmeg was for many years coveted by all the Europeans who had trading posts in Asia. In the fourteenth century a pound of nutmeg was as valuable as a cow. The Dutch had a monopoly on the nutmeg trade for years, but smuggling and wars dispersed the plants and the nutmeg tree spread to India and the Caribbean, and especially to Grenada.

Garam masala and certain curries contain nutmeg. Nutmeg is always used grated, for its aroma evaporates rapidly. It is used in pâtés, sausages, and salted meat and fish; it flavors vegetable purees, and it is also used on fresh pasta. It goes very well with pineapple, and it is surprising with chocolate. I use it on mozzarella when I don't have any basil.

My favorite recipes: Risotto of chestnuts and mushrooms with nutmeg; Macaroni salad with nutmeg.

Pepper: Poivre (black, green, and white)

Called *pippali* in Sanskrit (a name it shares with long pepper), in Latin it is *piper*. It was Pierre Poivre, governor of Mauritius, who gave it its French name (his own!). The spice originated on the Malabar coast in India. It exists in three principal forms: black, green, and white. All the peppercorns come from the same plant (of the Piperaceae family), but they are harvested at different stages of ripeness.

Black pepper is picked green, then fermented and dried in the sun. White pepper comes from ripe berries, dried in the sun without their husk. Green pepper is harvested earlier, in bunches; it is then cooked or preserved in vinegar or brine. You can also find it freeze-dried.

Undoubtedly, pepper is the queen of spices. The Romans appreciated it so much they thought it as valuable as gold. Rich people were even called "pepper sacks." Many medicinal and aphrodisiac qualities have been attributed to pepper. It is surely the most widely used spice in the world. It is found in all preserved meats and sausages. There is always a pepper mill on the table, to add taste to many dishes just before eating. Pepper can be used ground, crushed, or whole. Pepper sauce is one of the most widely known classic sauces.

My favorite recipes: Terrine of duck and green peppercorns; Cuttlefish with green peppercorns; Glazed mackerel with black pepper; Caramel jam with salt and pepper.

Peppers and Paprika: Piment et Paprika

The Latin word for peppers is *pigmentum*, from which comes the Spanish *pimiento*. The botanical name covers all the varieties of the species *Capsicum annuum*. The chili pepper, of the Solanaceae family (which includes many peppers, tamarillos, as well as flowers) comes from Latin America. The first seeds were brought to Europe by Christopher Columbus. They are so easy to grow that they quickly became one of the most used spices in the world. There are about two hundred varieties of peppers; each country has its local pepper and is proud of the dishes in which it is used. Some are very hot but don't have much flavor (such as Cayenne pepper); some (such as the sweet bell pepper) have a lot of flavor and are less hot; others succeed in combining flavor and strength (Espelette pepper, jalapeño, Hungarian cherry-pepper, habanero pepper). The Turks introduced the use of peppers in cooking in Europe. "Paprika" is a Hungarian word derived from the Ottoman *parapha*.

Peppers are used all over the world. They add spice to dishes in Asia as in Latin America. From France the Espelette pepper has gained an international reputation.

My favorite recipes: Cockles with Espelette pepper; Veal goulash with pistachios.

The French have two words for peppers: *piment* for chili peppers and *poivron* for sweet peppers. And, of course, peppercorns are *poivre*.—**TRANS.**

Poppy Seeds: Graines de Pavot

The poppy plant belongs to the Papaveraceae family (which includes more than two hundred herbs or plants with a milky sap). The botanical name is *Papaver somniferum*.

The poppy was first known for its analgesic and soporific qualities. The seeds are used in the cuisines of Eastern Europe, the Near East, and India. They are extracted from the flowers when ripe. First the latex containing the opium is removed from the flower heads. These are then dried in the sun, and the seeds harvested. The seeds have a light taste of hazelnut. They can be blue-gray, yellow, or white.

In Asia the seeds are used in some vegetable dishes and some curries. In Europe they are added to bread and some pastries. In the Near East, Turkey, and Eastern Europe they are made into a paste for a stuffing in some cakes.

I use poppy seeds in various dishes, both sweet and salty. They bring a very pleasant freshness and crunchiness.

My favorite recipes: Tomato tart with poppy seeds; Swordfish crusted with poppy seeds.

Ras el-hanout

This is a famous mixture of spices; the recipe, never standardized, reflects the baroque character of Moroccan cuisine. Its name literally means "the head of the shop," indicating that only one person in the shop is qualified to prepare this mixture according to the needs (and resources) of the customer. The mixture contains at least thirty spices, from the most common (cumin, turmeric, fenugreek, chili pepper, coriander, bay leaf, nutmeg, cinnamon, cardamom, clove) to the most unusual (rosebuds, tail-cubebe, seeds of paradise, Indian hemp, agnus-castus, fly cantharide). It is unlikely that commercial mixtures include all this; the odors vary enormously depending on what you can find. Trust your nose.

My favorite recipes: Terrine of chicken, sorrel, and Moroccan spices; Vegetable couscous with a spicy vinaigrette.

Saffron: Safran

The name comes from the Arabic *sahafaran* and the Persian *zafran*. The botanical name is *Crocus sativus*. The bulbous plant belongs to the Iradaceae family (the family of the iris and some perennial herbs) and comes from Asia Minor. The spice is the stigma of the purplish flower, which ripens in autumn.

Saffron was mentioned in some ancient Egyptian texts for its medicinal qualities. Later it conquered the Mediterranean basin, as can be seen in Greek mythology, especially the love affair of the nymph Smilax with Crocos (Smilax turned Crocos into the purple flower *Crocus sativus*, which produces saffron). Saffron was used in ancient Greece, then in Rome as a perfume and a dye. By the tenth century, apothecaries were middlemen in its spread to Europe. Arab merchants also helped spread the spice. Because of its commercial value, it was often faked when sold as powder. But anyone guilty of selling bogus saffron could be burned at the stake without a trial.

Saffron is now grown in Spain (the best comes from Castille), Greece, Turkey, and in Languedoc and the Gâtinas regions in France. It must be harvested by hand, which is why it is so costly when you consider that fifteen thousand stigmas are needed to get 4 ounces of spice. Its aroma is strong and its taste persists, so one must use it sparingly.

Saffron is used in the Mediterranean region, in paellas, Moroccan cuisine, bouillabaisse, and many other dishes. It is also common in northern India, and in pastries, ice creams, and crème anglaise. It is even found in very old recipes for English cakes.

My favorite recipes: Lemon soup with saffron; Wild mushroom mousse with saffron.

Sesame

This is certainly one of the oldest oleaginous (oil-producing) plants known and one of the spices most widely spread throughout the world. It is mentioned in the Bible and was used in the oldest known civilizations.

Sesamum indicum is from the Pedaliaceae family, related to the labieae (plants and herbs that often contain oil). It probably originated in tropical Africa. The tubular flowers produce pods containing many small white or black seeds, whose flavor is enhanced by light toasting. Koreans use the leaves, which are bitter, in marinades. The hazelnut flavor of toasted sesame makes it a universally loved spice. The seeds, with high energy value, are widely used in Mediterranean and oriental breads.

Sesame has many uses: halvah is a paste of sweetened sesame, and tahini is a sesame cream often used in dishes as a seasoning. The oil of toasted sesame seeds, dark brown in color and with a pronounced flavor, is much appreciated in China and Japan. This oil is never cooked, except when very diluted. Indian cuisine uses the raw sesame oil (gingelly oil), yellow in color and with a lighter flavor.

My favorite recipes: Tuna with white sesame seed crust; Two-sesame chocolate cream.

Star Anise: Anis étoilé (also called Badiane)

"Badiane" comes from the Persian, but this spice was first called *illicium* (in Latin, *illicere* means "to seduce"), then *illicium anisatum*. It has also been termed "Siberian anis" and "Chinese fennel."

It originates from China, and comes from a small shrub of the Magnoliaceae family. When ripe, the flowers form an eight-branched star (from which its Chinese name is taken). The shrub is a very archaic species, thought to originate in the distant past.

Star anise can be used whole or ground. Whole, it is used in court-bouillons (to cook crabs and lobsters) and marinades (for game). Ground, it can season white meats, but also can flavor chocolate (ganache).

My favorite recipes: Pollack with potatoes and star anise; Shoulder of lamb with star anise; Dark chocolate mousse with star anise.

Be sure you get Chinese star anise, as a similar plant, Japanese star anise, is highly toxic, according to the Food and Drug Agency.—**TRANS.**

Sumac

This oriental spice comes in the form of dark red powder that is extracted from the dried fruit of a tree (*Rhus coriaria*) belonging to the large family of sumacs widespread in Asia and America. In antiquity its refreshing, slightly acidic taste made it a valued condiment, but it fell from favor with the general adoption of lemon juice. Its German name *Essigbaum* ("vinegar tree") describes its virtues. It is used with fish but also, in the Near East, is sprinkled on rice and grilled meat. Sumac is often paired with raw onion for aperitif spices, and diluted in water to acidify solutions. In Jordan a mixture of spices called *zahtar* contains sesame, sumac, dried thyme, and salt.

My favorite recipes: Terrine of green peas and sumac; Olive oil with sumac; Pear, lime peel, and sumac jam.

Szechuan Pepper: Poivre de Sichuan

This spice is not a pepper but a reddish-brown berry that comes from a spiny Asian ash tree, the fagara. The berries are dried in the sun until they open. Only the coverings are harvested. The Chinese variety, with citrus and pepper aromas, is considered the best. The Japanese use the dried and crushed leaves of the fagara as a spicy condiment (*kona sanshô*), which they mix with dried seaweed and sesame to sprinkle on rice.

The Chinese use this spice a great deal. It is usually ground and mixed with fennel, star anise, cardamom, cinnamon, and cloves to make the famous mixture known as five spices.

I use Szechuan pepper very finely ground, for whole berries are too strong and overpowering. Grind Szechuan pepper at the last minute, as its flavors evaporate quickly. Use it at the end of cooking to retain all of its taste.

My favorite recipes: Soft-boiled eggs with Szechuan pepper; Sautéed white radish with Szechuan pepper; Spicy fish stew.

Tea: Thé

I use tea as a spice. I like to put in my dishes all sorts of flavorful teas, smoked or not smoked, black or green, and especially the powder of the Japanese green tea matcha, which has a strong perfume.

My favorite recipes: Duck legs braised with tea and cinnamon; Chocolate quenelles with jasmine.

Tonka Bean: Fève Tonka

This spice is little known outside the world of perfume. Its Latin name is *Dipteryx odorata* or *Coumarouna odorata*. It is the seed of a tropical tree (in Guyana and Venezuela, also Nigeria) and one of the main natural sources of coumarine, used in perfumes and cosmetics, and which has the odor of freshly mown hay. In Carib and Tupi, languages spoken in French Guyana and Venezuela, the tree is called *tonka* or *kumaru*, from which the name "coumarine" comes. The tonka bean is both soft and strong, like vanilla. Its taste is unique and incomparable. It is excellent in sweet dishes, but I like to use it with potatoes. Because it is toxic in high doses, it has become obsolete as a spice. But it takes very little tonka bean to flavor a dish; this fascinating spice deserves to be rediscovered.

My favorite recipes: Potato cakes with tonka beans and buckwheat; Mashed potatoes with tonka beans.

Be careful using tonka beans. They have been prohibited by the Food and Drug Administration for years but are available in France. We have used small quantities without any problem.—**TRANS.**

Turmeric: Curcuma

The word comes from Arabic *kourkoum*; the botanical name is *Curcuma longa*. It is a member of the Zingiberaceae family, a plant with rhizomes and pretty red flowers. It grows in India, Indonesia, and South America. Its flavor is both like nutmeg and like pepper.

In Indian medicine (and also in Western pharmaceutical preparations) turmeric is used as a powerful antiseptic digestive, and in India it is used for the skin. Fresh, it is a bright orange; dried, a saffron yellow. This makes it a substitute for saffron, although the flavor is quite different. Turmeric is used in many Indian dishes, and it is what makes curry powder yellow. It is also used in Moroccan cuisine. It is a strong coloring agent and is used as a dye for cloth.

My favorite recipes: Tomato and turmeric soup; Cauliflower cake with turmeric.

Vanilla: Vanille

This is a perennial plant of the Orchidaceae family, which grows along the sides of trees, a bit like ivy. Its botanical name is *Vanilla planifolia*, which comes from the Spanish *vainilla*, "little pod." The plant must be fertilized by pollen, which, in its region of origin (Mexico), is only carried by one kind of bee. In other regions (Madagascar, Réunion, Indonesia, the Caribbean) it must be fertilized artificially.

The plant was imported into Spain for the first time around 1550 by a Franciscan who had lived in Mexico. Europeans quickly took to it, first in chocolate and also as a powerful aphrodisiac. Originally the Aztecs used it to flavor chocolate by crushing the beans with the pods. The characteristic flavor of vanilla comes from the small black seeds enclosed in the pod. You must split the pod and scrape the seeds to reveal its marvelous perfume.

After a series of fermentations and drying, vanilla is put on the market. The plant is only productive after four years, when about fifty pods can be harvested. When ripe these measure about seven to ten inches. In the French Caribbean the largest pods are called "vanillons."

Vanilla is primarily used in sweet dishes, but sometimes it can flavor delicately savory dishes (scallops, lobsters, white meats).

My favorite recipes: White meat turkey salad with vanilla oil; Peanut oil infused with vanilla.

Wasabi

This has been called "Japanese mustard" or "Japanese horseradish." This fine green paste, smelling like fiery mustard, comes from the root and part of the stem of a cross-shaped water plant with large leaves, *Wasabia japonica*. This is an exclusively Japanese spice, used especially with raw fish and sushi. It is very difficult to cultivate, and part of the yield still comes from wild plants. In Japan it is sometimes used fresh, but in other countries it is often available only in powdered form and must be diluted with a little water to form a paste.

Its flavor is so strong that *namiru* ("tears") is a popular name for wasabi. This flavor only comes out after a few minutes when you add water; if you taste the powder it will simply seem bitter.

My favorite recipe: Sautéed hake with wasabi.

You can buy wasabi in a tube in most supermarkets.—**TRANS.**

Translators' notes on other ingredients, sometimes difficult to find in the United States, and possible substitutions

Salt: Fleur de sel, sel de Guérande, and gros sel

Fleur de sel is gathered from the sea in Brittany at Guérande, on the Île de Ré and at Aigues-Mortes in the Camarge. It is an ultra-fine salt crust, only 3 to 4 percent of the salt production. It has a very distinct texture. It is very delicate and is never used in cooking, but for seasoning at the table. For cooking, Delacourcelle uses sel de Guérande for a coarser form of this sea salt. These salts are available in the United States but are rather expensive. For both these and for gros sel (a term Delacourcelle sometimes uses to mean coarse salt) you could substitute kosher salt. It is not as fine, of course, but much cheaper.

Crème fraîche

Crème fraîche (a thickened, fermented cream) can now be purchased in the United States, either imported or made in California and Vermont. As a substitute you can use a mixture of cream and sour cream or yogurt. (To avoid curdling either sour cream or yogurt, do not cover the pan while cooking or add them to boiling liquid.) Another substitute can be made by adding 1 tablespoon of buttermilk to 1 cup whipping cream, leaving this in a warm place for at least 8 hours, then refrigerating. Delacourcelle measures light crème fraîche by volume but thick crème fraîche by weight. He also uses liquid cream, which is heavy cream, closer to American whipping cream.

Belle de Fontenay and Charlotte potatoes

These can sometimes be obtained in England and in the United States. They are large and pale yellow, with a waxy rather than floury texture. They are recommended for salads or as steamed or browned potatoes. Substitute a good waxy potato, perhaps a new potato.

Index of Spices

Index of Recipes

IN THE AT TABLE SERIES

Spiced
Recipes from Le Pré Verre
Philippe Delacourcelle
Translated and with a preface by
Adele King and Bruce King

Eating in Eden
Food and American Utopias
Edited by Etta M. Madden and
Martha L. Finch

Recovering Our Ancestors' Gardens
Indigenous Recipes and Guide to
Diet and Fitness
Devon Abbott Mihesuah

Dueling Chefs
A Vegetarian and a Meat Lover
Debate the Plate
Maggie Pleskac and
Sean Carmichael

A Taste of Heritage
Crow Indian Recipes
and Herbal Medicines
Alma Hogan Snell
Edited by Lisa Castle

AVAILABLE IN BISON BOOKS EDITIONS

The Food and Cooking of
Eastern Europe
Lesley Chamberlain
With a new introduction
by the author

The Food and Cooking of Russia
Lesley Chamberlain
With a new introduction
by the author

Masters of American Cookery
M. F. K. Fisher, James Beard,
Craig Claiborne, Julia Child
Betty Fussell
With a preface by the author

Good Things
Jane Grigson

Jane Grigson's Fruit Book
Jane Grigson
New introduction by
Sara Dickerman

Jane Grigson's Vegetable Book
Jane Grigson
New introduction by Amy Sherman

Dining with Marcel Proust
A Practical Guide to French Cuisine
of the Belle Epoque
Shirley King
Foreword by James Beard

Pampille's Table
Recipes and Writings from the
French Countryside from Marthe
Daudet's Les Bons Plats de France
Translated and adapted by
Shirley King